DEADLY DISEASES AND EPIDEMICS

LUNG CANCER

DEADLY DISEASES AND EPIDEMICS

DEADLY DISEASES AND EPIDEMICS

LUNG CANCER

Carmen Ferreiro

FOUNDING EDITOR
The Late I. Edward Alcamo
Distinguished Teaching Professor of Microbiology,
SUNY Farmingdale

FOREWORD BY
David Heymann
World Health Organization

CHELSEA HOUSE
PUBLISHERS
An imprint of Infobase Publishing

Dedicated to Ed Alcamo

Lung Cancer

Copyright © 2007 by Infobase Publishing

All rights reserved. No part of this book may be reproduced or utilized in any form or by any means, electronic or mechanical, including photocopying, recording, or by any information storage or retrieval systems, without permission in writing from the publisher. For information contact:

Chelsea House
An imprint of Infobase Publishing
132 West 31st Street
New York, NY 10001

Library of Congress Cataloging-in-Publication Data
Ferreiro, Carmen.
    Lung cancer / Carmen Ferreiro ; consulting editor, I. Edward Alcamo ; foreword by David Heymann.
        p. cm. — (Deadly diseases and epidemics)
    Includes bibliographical references and index.
    ISBN 0-7910-8937-1 (hc : alk. paper)
    1. Lungs—Cancer—Juvenile literature. I. Alcamo, I. Edward. II. title. III. Series.
    RC280.L8F47 2006
    616.99'424—dc22   2006010422

Chelsea House books are available at special discounts when purchased in bulk quantities for businesses, associations, institutions, or sales promotions. Please call our Special Sales Department in New York at (212) 967-8800 or (800) 322-8755.

You can find Chelsea House on the World Wide Web at http://www.chelseahouse.com

Series design by Terry Mallon
Cover design by Keith Trego

Printed in the United States of America

Bang EJB 10 9 8 7 6 5 4 3 2 1

This book is printed on acid-free paper.

All links and Web addresses were checked and verified to be correct at the time of publication. Because of the dynamic nature of the Web, some addresses and links may have changed since publication and may no longer be valid.

Neovostat is a registered trademark of AEterna. Zyban is a registered trademark of GlaxoSmithKline. Uvadex is a registered trademark of Therakos, Inc.

Table of Contents

Foreword

In the 1960s, many of the infectious diseases that had terrorized generations were tamed. After a century of advances, the leading killers of Americans both young and old were being prevented with new vaccines or cured with new medicines. The risk of death from pneumonia, tuberculosis (TB), meningitis, influenza, whooping cough, and diphtheria declined dramatically. New vaccines lifted the fear that summer would bring polio, and a global campaign was on the verge of eradicating smallpox worldwide. New pesticides like DDT cleared mosquitoes from homes and fields, thus reducing the incidence of malaria, which was present in the southern United States and which remains a leading killer of children worldwide. New technologies produced safe drinking water and removed the risk of cholera and other water-borne diseases. Science seemed unstoppable. Disease seemed destined to all but disappear.

But the euphoria of the 1960s has evaporated.

The microbes fought back. Those causing diseases like TB and malaria evolved resistance to cheap and effective drugs. The mosquito developed the ability to defuse pesticides. New diseases emerged, including AIDS, Legionnaires', and Lyme disease. And diseases which had not been seen in decades reemerged, as the hantavirus did in the Navajo Nation in 1993. Technology itself actually created new health risks. The global transportation network, for example, meant that diseases like West Nile virus could spread beyond isolated regions and quickly become global threats. Even modern public health protections sometimes failed, as they did in 1993 in Milwaukee, Wisconsin, resulting in 400,000 cases of the digestive system illness cryptosporidiosis. And, more recently, the threat from smallpox, a disease believed to be completely eradicated, has returned along with other potential bioterrorism weapons such as anthrax.

The lesson is that the fight against infectious diseases will never end.

In our constant struggle against disease, we as individuals have a weapon that does not require vaccines or drugs, and that is the warehouse of knowledge. We learn from the history of science that "modern" beliefs can be wrong. In this series of books, for example, you will learn that diseases like syphilis were once thought to be caused by eating potatoes. The invention of the microscope set science on the right path. There are more positive lessons from history. For example, smallpox was eliminated by vaccinating everyone who had come in contact with an infected person. This "ring" approach to smallpox control is still the preferred method for confronting an outbreak, should the disease be intentionally reintroduced.

At the same time, we are constantly adding new drugs, new vaccines, and new information to the warehouse. Recently, the entire human genome was decoded. So too was the genome of the parasite that causes malaria. Perhaps by looking at the microbe and the victim through the lens of genetics we will be able to discover new ways to fight malaria, which remains the leading killer of children in many countries.

Because of advances in our understanding of such diseases as AIDS, entire new classes of antiretroviral drugs have been developed. But resistance to all these drugs has already been detected, so we know that AIDS drug development must continue.

Education, experimentation, and the discoveries that grow out of them are the best tools to protect health. Opening this book may put you on the path of discovery. I hope so, because new vaccines, new antibiotics, new technologies, and, most importantly, new scientists are needed now more than ever if we are to remain on the winning side of this struggle against microbes.

David Heymann
Executive Director
Communicable Diseases Section
World Health Organization
Geneva, Switzerland

1

Cancer and the Lungs

Lung cancer is a swift killer. Of the 172,570 people who were diagnosed with lung cancer in the United States in 2005[1] only 15 percent[2] will survive for five years.

Lung cancer is the third most common type of cancer in the United States (after prostate cancer and breast cancer). Yet due to its bleak outcome, it is the number-one killer among cancer patients. According to the American Lung Association, lung cancer caused an estimated 160,440 deaths in 2004, accounting for 28.5 percent of all cancer-related deaths.[3]

These statistics are even more shocking when we consider that at the beginning of the twentieth century[4] lung cancer was virtually an unknown disease.

But lung cancer can be stopped.

Unlike other forms of cancer that strike seemingly at random or are linked to a **genetic susceptibility** (hereditary trait) we can do nothing about—at least not for the moment, many studies have demonstrated the direct correlation between smoking and lung cancer. The American Lung Association estimates that smoking causes 90 percent of cases of lung cancer. This means that the power to stop lung cancer before it starts is quite literally in our hands.

WHAT IS CANCER?

The word *cancer* comes from the Greek word *karkinos* meaning *crab*. Hippocrates, the great Greek physician (460-370 B.C.) who is considered the father of modern medicine, gave it this name because the **tumors** that are the visible evidence of many types of cancer reminded him of a crab, with a central body (the tumor or lump) from which several rays—the legs—spread into the surrounding tissue.[5]

Cancer is an ancient disease. Mummies some 2,500 years old have been discovered in Peru with lumps that clearly suggest cancer as the cause of death. Pictures found in the walls of ancient Egyptian tombs depict human figures with tumors.

Yet until the twentieth century cancer was a rare disease. One of the reasons for this is that cancer needs time to grow, which means that it appears predominantly in older people. Until recently, not many people lived to old age. They were more likely to die young from accidents, malnutrition, hard physical work, infectious diseases, and, in the case of women, childbirth.

During the twentieth century the discovery of antibiotics, better nutrition, and general improvement in work conditions and health care helped eliminate many of these causes of death. With more people living longer, the number of cases of cancer increased.

TYPES OF CANCERS

Cancer is a general term for abnormal **cell** division and growth. This means cancer is not a single disease but many—as many as there are different types of cells in the human body. In medical terms, the 150 or so different cancers that have been found to date are grouped into five types, according to the kind of **tissue** in which they develop. These types are carcinoma, sarcoma, leukemia, lymphoma, and myeloma.[6]

Carcinomas are cancers that develop in the **epithelial cells** that cover the skin, mouth, nose, throat, and lung airways, as well as the genitourinary and gastrointestinal (GI) tracts. They also cover glands such as the breast and thyroid. Carcinomas are tumors. The most common carcinomas are in the lung, breast, prostate, skin, stomach, and colon.

Sarcomas form in bones or in soft connective and supportive tissues such as cartilage, muscles, tendons, fat, and the outer lining of the lungs, abdomen, heart, central nervous system, and blood vessels. Since soft tissues can be found in every **organ**, sarcomas can occur anywhere in the body. Sarcomas are also tumors.

Leukemias, lymphomas, and myelomas are *not* tumors.

Leukemias are a group of cancers of the cells of the blood and **bone marrow** (the soft part inside the bones where blood cells originate). There are three types of blood cells: red blood cells that transport oxygen; platelets that protect against bruising and bleeding; and white blood cells, or **leukocytes,** that fight infections. Leukemias are characterized by an abnormal production of leukocytes. Depending on the type of leukocytes that become cancerous, leukemias are classified as myeloid or lymphoid, terms which derive from two types of leukocytes, the **neutrophils** and **lymphocytes**.

Myeloid cells help form neutrophils, which are the leukocytes that play a role in the early stages of the body's defense against **microorganisms**. Neutrophils are **macrophages**; that is, they engulf and eliminate foreign matter, bacteria, and debris from cells that have been destroyed by infection. Lymphoid cells give rise to **lymphocytes**, the leukocytes that make up the second line of the body's defense against foreign molecules.

Lymphomas, as you'll learn below, usually occur when lymphocytes grow out of control.

Leukemias are also classified as acute or chronic. Acute leukemias are more aggressive and can quickly lead to death. Without rapid treatment, most patients will die in days or weeks. Chronic leukemias grow more slowly and may not cause obvious problems for years.

Lymphomas are cancers that develop in the lymphatic system, a basic part of the **immune system** defending the body against disease. The lymphatic system consists of a complex network of channels that carries **lymph**, a fluid rich in different types of leukocytes, or white blood cells. The lymphocytes are found either clustered in **lymph nodes,** or **glands,** or circulating through the bloodstream and in **lymphatic vessels**. When a lymphoma develops, the lymph glands or other organs swell where healthy lymphocytes are normally found, and lumps appear throughout the body.

One specific kind of lymphoma is called Hodgkin's disease. All other kinds are referred to as non-Hodgkin's lymphomas. There are many varieties of both Hodgkin's disease and non-Hodgkin's lymphomas.

Multiple myeloma is a cancer of the plasma cell, a type of B lymphocyte responsible for producing **antibodies** (complex proteins that fight infection). Myeloma is a rare disease (1 percent of all cases of cancer) characterized by the growth of **malignant** plasma cells, mostly in the bone marrow.

IS A TUMOR ALWAYS A CANCER?

Not all tumors are cancer. A tumor is a mass of cells that does not belong to the tissue where it is growing and has no function. Some, like freckles, moles, and warts, are harmless. Harmless tumors are called benign. Cells in a benign tumor look and act more like normal cells. They are differentiated, which means they become a specific type of cell and will grow and spread more slowly than undifferentiated cells. Benign tumors grow slowly and do not move from the place where they have formed. Because they are usually encapsulated by connective tissue, they have smooth edges.

Cancers are malignant tumors: tumors with no clear-cut borders, in which the cells divide with no control, invade surrounding tissues, develop a network of blood vessels to get nourishment, and eventually spread to other places in the body.

Not all types of cancer form tumors. In leukemias, for instance, the cancer cells are abnormal white blood cells, or leukocytes, that circulate freely in the bloodstream.

Lung cancer is a carcinoma that affects the lungs. The role of the lungs is to draw oxygen from the air and to expel toxic carbon dioxide. Every cell in our body needs oxygen to stay alive. Without oxygen, we would die in minutes. When the lungs do not work properly, every part of the body suffers. That is why lung cancer is such a deadly disease.

To understand lung cancer, we need to know the anatomy of the lungs and how they work.

HOW DO THE LUNGS WORK?

Single-celled organisms like amoebas move freely and take the oxygen they need from their surroundings. But for multicellular organisms such as humans, trillions of cells that make up our bodies need oxygen yet most of them cannot move. To solve this problem, we have a complex circuit of vessels with specialized cells that carry oxygen throughout the body wherever it is needed.

This circuit is called the circulatory system; the specialized cells are red blood cells. Pumped by the heart, blood moves through the body, carrying oxygen and removing carbon dioxide (CO_2), the toxic waste of all the reactions that take place inside the cells. The blood cells use up the oxygen they are carrying, bind to new oxygen molecules, and get rid of CO_2 in a gas exchange that takes place in the lungs.

The lungs are located in the chest cavity, in the upper part of the torso (the central part of the body). They are separated from the stomach and other organs of the lower part of the torso by a flat muscle called the diaphragm. The diaphragm moves up and down as we breathe, pushing used CO_2 out of the lungs and then drawing in new oxygen.

We have two lungs. The right lung has three sections called lobes. The left one has only two lobes and is smaller because the heart is located there. Each lobe is in itself a mini-lung. If some lobes are removed, the others are still able to function on their own.

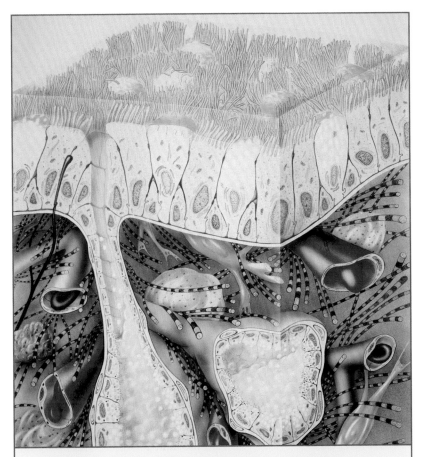

Figure 1.1 Artist's rendering of cells lining a bronchus in a lung. Cross-section of an epithelial cell with conjunctive tissue and bronchial cell secreting mucus. © Michael Gilles/Photo Researchers, Inc.

The air we inhale through the nose or mouth goes into the windpipe or trachea. Inside the chest, the trachea divides into two branches, or **bronchi**, one for each lung. Each of the bronchi then divides again into a total of five branches, one for each of the five lobes. Inside each lobe, these branches divide again and again into more delicate branches called bronchioles.

1.2 Structure of the Lungs

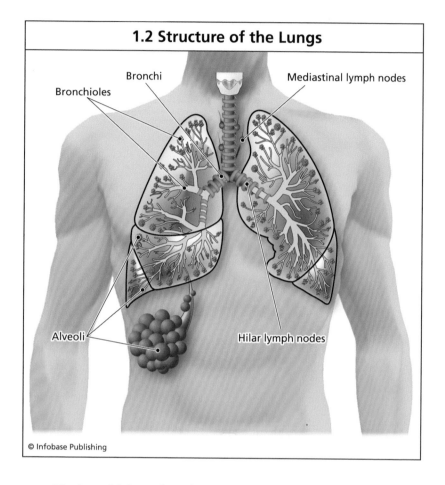

Bronchi

Bronchioles

Mediastinal lymph nodes

Alveoli

Hilar lymph nodes

© Infobase Publishing

The bronchioles end in clusters of microscopic air sacs called **alveoli.** You can think of the lungs as an inverted broccoli floret.

The alveoli are surrounded by thin blood vessels called **capillaries** (from the Latin word for *hair*). When the air comes into the lungs, the alveoli expand like tiny balloons. The transfer of oxygen and carbon dioxide takes place through the thin, elastic walls of the alveoli and capillaries.

LUNGS' DEFENSES AND DISEASE

Because of their nature, the lungs are in direct contact with the air. This makes them extremely vulnerable to any pollutants that may be in the air. To help protect the lungs against pollutants, the body has developed several defense mechanisms.

Mucus (the sticky fluid secreted by the epithelial cells that line your nose and bronchial tubes) and the cilia (microscopic hairs that grow in their walls) are the first line of defense. Every time we breathe, mucus traps dirt and germs from the air, and cilia send them down your throat. When we swallow, saliva carries mucus into your digestive system for eventual disposal.

Another line of defense that helps protect the lungs from the environment is the lymphatic system. As we have discussed earlier, lymph is a fluid rich in white blood cells that circulates through a system of lymphatic vessels. In many places, including around the lungs, this network is dotted with lymph nodes, or glands.

The leukocytes are the body's army against disease. Some leukocytes work by gobbling up the offending agents. Others make antibodies, which are complex proteins that bind to and kill germs.

Under normal circumstances, these defenses are enough to protect the lungs. But when the lungs are chronically exposed to pollutants, the glands that produce mucus go into overdrive. They produce more and more mucus as they try to get rid of the irritant particles. But the cilia in the airways, which are also damaged by these same pollutants, cannot keep up with the excess mucus. As a consequence mucus accumulates, making it easy for infection to develop.

As is always the case when there is an infection, the body sends leukocytes to fight it. This causes the airways and alveoli to become inflamed. The inflammation thickens the walls, making them less elastic and less able to eliminate mucus.

Mucus accumulation and inflammation of the airways make breathing difficult and lead to coughing. Sometimes they cause pneumonia, an infection of the lungs caused by bacteria that can be treated with antibiotics. If the causes of the irritation are not removed, there is a large chance that disease will

1.3 The Development and

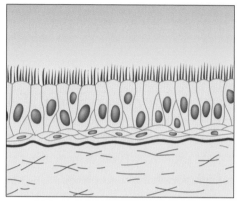

Healthy tissue
The cells that line the airways look like tall columns. Some secrete mucus, which traps harmful particles from the air. Others grow hair-like cilia, which sweep away debris.

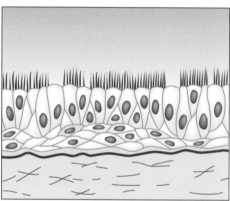

Hyperplasia
Genetic damage has occurred. Cells begin to divide more rapidly than usual. At first, the new cells appear normal or close to normal.

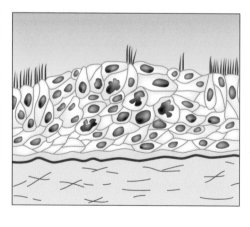

Dysplasia
At this stage, cells have de-differentiated. New cells look less like healthy airway cells; some are flat and wide instead of tall and narrow. They may lack cilia, so they can't perform their normal protective functions.

Spread of Lung Cancer

Tumor
Cells have become cancerous and have formed a tumor. Angiogenesis has begun: the tumor is developing a network of new blood vessels to sustain its growth. Depending on its location and size, the tumor may cause symptoms.

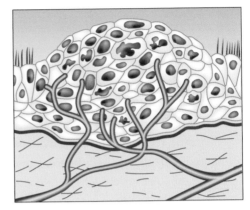

Invasive tumor
The cancer has spread beyond its original site. It may grow into the chest wall, the mediastinum (space between the lungs), or adjacent lobes of the lung.

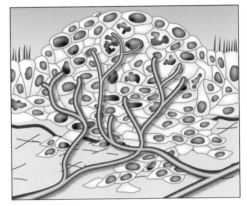

Metastatic cancer
Cancerous cells have broken off and migrated elsewhere in the body via the bloodstream or lymphatic system. Lung cancer can travel to any organ, but it most often spreads to the bones, the brain, the liver, and the adrenal glands.

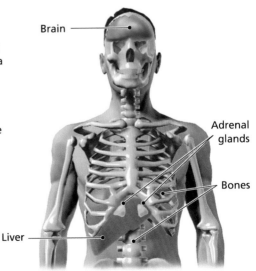

Brain

Adrenal glands

Bones

Liver

occur again. Chronic bronchitis and emphysema may also develop.

Repeated infections lead to scarring. Scars narrow the airways that are already clogged with excess mucus, making breathing even more difficult. As the person struggles to breathe, the soft walls of the bronchioles collapse, causing the typical symptoms of chronic bronchitis: shortness of breath and fatigue.

With emphysema, the irritants cause the alveoli to become less elastic, reducing their capacity to move air in and out of the lungs. Eventually the walls between the alveoli collapse, diminishing the total surface for the interchange of oxygen and carbon dioxide. Symptoms of emphysema include a feeling of tightness in the chest and shortness of breath.

Most smokers develop both chronic bronchitis and emphysema. Together, these create a condition called **chronic obstructive pulmonary disease** (COPD). COPD is a serious disease that kills more than 100,000 people each year. COPD sufferers should be aware that the irritants that cause COPD also cause cancer. In fact, the symptoms of both diseases overlap.

LUNG CANCER

Lung cancer is a carcinoma, an abnormal growth that usually starts in the epithelial cells that line the bronchial tubes or the alveoli.

The first step in the development of a tumor is **hyperplasia,** that is, a rapid increase in the number of cells. Rapid cell division does not always produce a tumor. For instance, rapid cell division occurs during the development of the embryo or during the healing of a wound. The difference in these two examples is that once the growth or healing is finished, the cells stop dividing. Cancer cells, on the other hand, continue to divide in an uncontrolled way.

Under a microscope normal epithelial lung cells look like tall columns. At first precancerous cells look like the healthy cells, but as their divisions continue, the new cells start to look less and less like the original tall narrow cells. They may be flat and wide and lack cilia. This process of **de-differentiation** (a loss of **differentiation**, which is the healthy process by which new cells acquire specialized capabilities) is called **dysplasia**. Dysplastic cells can no longer perform the tasks the normal cells do. They cannot secrete mucus or dispose of it because they don't have cilia.

These two processes—hyperplasia and dysplasia—are considered the premalignant **stages** of cancer, and they can take decades to develop. Eventually the de-differentiated cells form a tumor, or a mass of abnormal tissue. Like any other cells, the cells in the tumor need the bloodstream to provide them with nourishment. To continue growing, the tumor must develop a network of new blood vessels that will reach all its cells. This pathological process is called **angiogenesis**.

Once the tumor has developed its own network of blood vessels, its cells can migrate to other sites. Sometimes, the tumor cells invade nearby tissues. For instance, lung cancer tumors can intrude into the chest wall, the **mediastinum** (space between the lungs), or into adjacent lung lobes. In other cases, cancerous cells break away from the original tumor and travel to other parts of the body through the bloodstream or lymphatic system. The process of migration of cancer cells is called **metastasis**. Once there, they produce a secondary tumor. The places where lung cancer is most likely to spread are the bones, the brain, the liver, and the adrenal glands.

Although it is still not completely understood, all cancers are a disease in which cells act abnormally. To understand what cancer is and how it happens, we first need to understand how normal cells behave.

2

Cancer and the Cell

Cancer is not an infectious disease. It is not caused by a microorganism that has somehow broken into the body and then multiplied once inside. Cancer is a cellular disease, a disease in which cells grow and divide out of control.

NORMAL CELL, CANCER CELL

Normal cells grow and divide, too. In fact, the trillions of cells that make up the human body all come from a single cell: the fertilized egg. Right after fertilization, the egg divides into two cells, and these two cells divide into four, and then into eight and so on (Figure 2.1). After dividing 10 times, that single cell has produced 1,204 cells; after 15 divisions, there are 32,768 cells.[7]

At first, all the cells are identical. As the embryo develops, however, they start to specialize. They become elongated muscle cells, tall skin cells, or star-shaped astrocytes (a type of brain cell). Their different shapes reflect molecular changes that will allow them to perform their specific functions. Some of these specialized cells, such as nerve cells, stop dividing once the nervous system is mature. Others, including blood and skin cells, continue to divide throughout a person's lifetime.[8]

Soon specialized cells group to form tissues, which in turn collaborate with one another to form a complex, interdependent, mutually supporting community: a functional organism.

We might envision the human body as an ecosystem whose individual members are cells.[9] But unlike other ecosystems, where survival of the fittest is the rule, the cells of the body work together to survive. To do this, the cells send, receive, and follow a complex set of signals. These signals

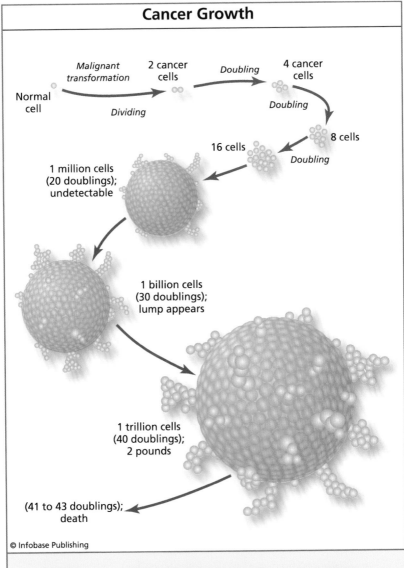

Figure 2.1 The malignant transformation of a normal cell and subsequent doublings. After twenty doublings (1 million cancer cells), the cancer is still too small to detect.

tell them when to rest, divide, differentiate, or die—whatever is needed for the good of the organism as a whole.

Cancer cells are an exception. Cancer cells do not follow orders; they act independently, disregarding the needs of the community of cells around them. Cancer cells take available nutrients and grow and divide unchecked, forming a tumor.

Eventually the cancer cells run out of food or out of space and start competing with one another, pushing aside the nearby normal tissue. Sometimes some of the cells in the tumor break off and move through blood or lymph to distant sites in the body, where they form new tumors. As body tissues are invaded and shoved aside to make room for growing tumors, the body's ecosystem collapses. Cancer cells that seem unstoppable die, too.

But what causes this transformation of normal cells to cancer cells? What makes cancer cells ignore orders from their neighbors and continue to grow and divide even when no more cells are needed? To answer these questions, we must look inside the cell's nucleus into the complex molecule called **DNA**, which carries the instructions for everything the cell does.

GENES AND CHROMOSOMES

It started with peas—yellow and green peas—and a monk who loved math and wanted to be a teacher but failed the test to become one. Instead he bred plants in the garden of his monastery in the middle of the nineteenth century in what is now the Slovak Republic. His name was Gregor Johann Mendel.

Mendel was a hard worker and a careful scientist. He developed dozens of varieties of many different plants before choosing the pea plant as his subject of study. The 34 pure strains of pea plants he developed differed from one another in ways that were easy to see and classify. One of the differences between two of these strains was the color of their seeds. One of the strains always had green seeds; the other had yellow seeds.[10]

Figure 2.2 Gregor Mendel. Courtesy of the National Library of Medicine

At the time Mendel was experimenting with plants, biologists thought offspring inherited a mix, or an average, of the traits of their parents. They believed, for instance, that if your father were tall and your mother short, you would be of aver-age height. Mendel's results challenged this notion. When he crossbred plants with green seeds and plants with yellow seeds, the first generation had yellow seeds. However, the green-seed characteristic had not vanished entirely. Green seeds reap-peared in the next generation of plants in a mathematical pro-portion of three yellow-seeded plants to one green-seeded plant.

To Mendel, the conclusion of these experiments was obvi-ous: Parental traits were not blended, but instead were passed to descendants as discrete packages of information, or **genes**. All the plants of the first generation received two genes, Mendel concluded, one from each parent. One gene told the pea to be yellow, and the other told it to be green. Somehow the yellow always won.

In the second generation, some plants received two green genes (one from each parent) and became green, while plants that received either one or two yellow genes were yellow. In other words, yellow was a **dominant trait** (only one yellow gene was needed for the plant to be yellow), and green was a **recessive trait** (the plant needed two green genes to become green).

Mendel presented a mathematical analysis of his results to the Brunn Natural Science Society in 1865. No one in the audi-ence could make sense of what they thought was Mendel's mathematical gibberish. Although his results were published the following year in the Society's proceedings, no one under-stood their significance until the beginning of the twentieth century.

By then the optical microscope had allowed scientists to see that every plant and animal is made of cells, but also to look inside these cells. Among the things they had seen were **chro-mosomes**, rod-like structures that became visible in the nucleus of the cell when the cell was getting ready to divide. Chromosomes always came in pairs in the **somatic cells** (the

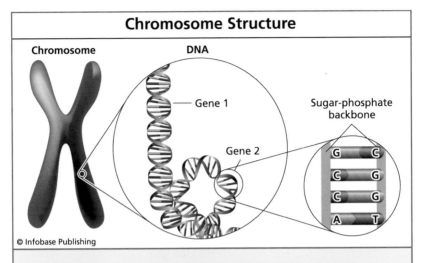

Chromosome Structure

Chromosome

DNA

Gene 1

Sugar-phosphate backbone

Gene 2

© Infobase Publishing

Figure 2.3 In eukaryotic cells, the genetic material exists in several linear molecules of deoxyribonucleic acid (DNA). These linear DNA molecules are associated with proteins that form the chromosomes. A DNA molecule is made of nucleotides. Each nucleotide contains a sugar, a phosphate, and one of four nitrogen bases. Each DNA molecule contains many different genes.

cells that form the body)—one pair from the mother and one from the father. Human cells have 23 pairs of chromosomes.

Just before the formation of the **gametes** (the sexual cells), each pair of chromosomes binds together and then splits into separate cells. This way, each gamete receives a complete set of chromosomes. But this set is not the set that originally came from the father or the mother but is a mixture of the two. One cell may have chromosomes 1, 5, 7 and 20 from the mother and the remaining 19 from the father, or any other possible combination.

In 1903, three American cell biologists named W. A. Cannon, Edmund Wilson, and Walter Sutton pointed out the similarities between chromosomes and genes.[11] Both genes and chromosomes occur in pairs, with one member of the pair from the female parent and the other from the male parent.

Both genes and chromosome pairs are separated when gametes are formed and then reunited at the time of fertilization. The three biologists reached the conclusion that the genes are carried in the chromosomes and that genes transmit hereditary information. Because there are more genes than chromosomes, they inferred that each chromosome contains many genes. They were right. We know now that in the human cell, for instance, there are about 30,000 genes,[12] and only 23 pairs of chromosomes.

Commonly inherited traits include things like hair color and texture, eye color and facial structure, build, and diseases such as hemophilia and hypertension.

THE GENETIC CODE

By the middle of the twentieth century scientists generally accepted that chromosomes are made of **proteins** and deoxyribonucleic acid (DNA) and that, of the two, DNA is responsible for carrying the genetic information. How DNA, a molecule made in fixed proportions of sugar, phosphate, and

CANCER IS GENETIC BUT NOT HEREDITARY

Cancer is a genetic disease. Yet most cancers are not hereditary. Cancer is genetic because it is the result of mutations or alterations in the DNA. These mutations are usually acquired during the life of the individual in his or her somatic cells, and are *not* transmitted to the person's offspring. When the body dies, all the somatic cells die, too, including the cancerous cells. However, a few mutations do occur in the reproductive cells, producing oncogenes (meaning *tumor* from the Greek word *oncos*), and as a consequence may be passed on to a person's descendants. A person who inherits these mutations has an increased likelihood of developing cancer.

Figure 2.4 Scientist James Watson stands beside a model of the DNA double helix, which he discovered with Francis Crick, at an exhibit in Berlin in October 2004. © AP/Wide World Photos

four different **bases**—adenine (A), thymine (T), cytosine (C), and guanine (G)—was able to store information was still a mystery.

James Watson and Francis Crick brilliantly answered this puzzling question in 1953.[13] In their theory the structure of the DNA in the chromosomes consists of two chains twisted around each other in the form of a double helix (Figure 2.4).

The double helix is like a rope ladder that is continually twisted. Its two upright ladders are made of alternating molecules of sugar and phosphate, while the rungs face one another, consisting of two of the four available nitrogenous bases (A, T, C, or G). Each chromosome consists of thousands and thousands of rungs.

In this model the mysterious **genetic code** is the language used by cells to pass information to the next generation. It is stored as a long sequence of bases in the DNA strand. A typical sequence might be ATTAGCGCCACTACG.

Because the molecules of adenine and guanine are larger than thymine and cytosine, only two combinations would allow a pair of bases to fit into the double helix: A facing T and G facing C (Figure 2.5). This restriction in the base pairing means that the sequence of bases in one of the strands of the double helix had to be complementary to the one in the opposite strand. Watson and Crick realized that this restriction provides a way for the DNA to replicate, or duplicate itself. During replication, the double helix opens like a zipper and each of its strands forms a complementary copy of itself by binding to free **nucleotides**.

For the cell to be able to use the information stored in the DNA, this information must be first translated into protein molecules. This process is twofold. First, the long strand of DNA is copied into shorter, single-stranded chains of a different nucleic acid called mRNA (messenger ribonucleic acid). Each chain of mRNA serves as the template for a specific protein. Then, the mRNA leaves the nucleus and is translated in

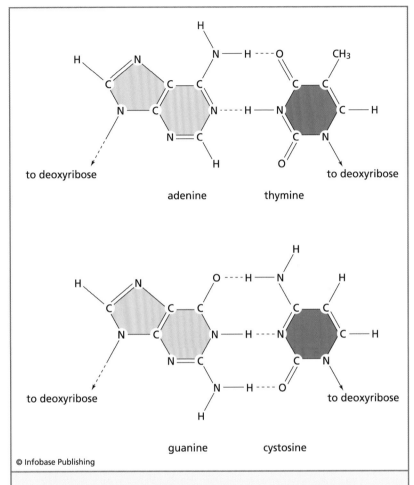

to deoxyribose   to deoxyribose

adenine   thymine

to deoxyribose   to deoxyribose

guanine   cystosine

© Infobase Publishing

Figure 2.5 The A-T (adenine-thymine) and G-C (guanine-cyto-sine) base pairs of DNA, as seen from one end of a DNA mole-cule. Dotted lines designate hydrogen bonds.

the **cytoplasm** into a sequence of **amino acids** (the building blocks of proteins.) (See Figure 2.6.)

The translation of the mRNA into proteins is a complex process that requires protein "assembly machines" known as ribosomes and another strand of **RNA**, called **tRNA**. Different

Transcription and Translation

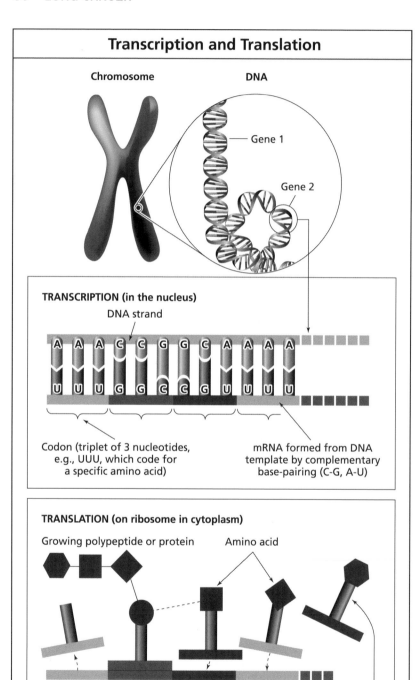

Chromosome

DNA

Gene 1

Gene 2

TRANSCRIPTION (in the nucleus)

DNA strand

Codon (triplet of 3 nucleotides, e.g., UUU, which code for a specific amino acid)

mRNA formed from DNA template by complementary base-pairing (C-G, A-U)

TRANSLATION (on ribosome in cytoplasm)

Growing polypeptide or protein

Amino acid

tRNA specific for amino acid and mRNA codon

mRNA

tRNA molecules carry the amino acids, one at a time, to the ribosomes in the order specified by the sequence of nucleotides that makes up the mRNA, until the protein is fully assembled.

Proteins have different functions in the cell. Some are structural proteins; they build the cell. Others are hormones serving as growth factors, or **cytokines**, which exit the cell and carry messages to other cells. Some are enzymes; they catalyze all the chemical reactions that take place in the cell. Still others are regulatory proteins that may, among other actions, control the function of other proteins, regulate the process of DNA replication, or tell genes when to turn on or turn off. When a gene is on, it will be copied into a messenger RNA (mRNA) and eventually translated into a protein.

The process of DNA replication is not entirely precise. Sometimes mistakes are made and the wrong base is incorporated into the DNA strand. If the mistake, or **mutation**, happens to occur in the sequence of a gene that is being translated into a protein, it can cause the protein to be defective or nonfunctional. If it happens in the regulatory sequence of the gene—the part of the gene that controls **gene expression**—the mutation can cause the gene to be on all the time. If the mutation affects the genes that control cell division and creates a cell that disobeys the normal restrictions on cell proliferation, cancer might develop.

Figure 2.6 (left) Transcription is the way in which genes are copied into RNA. During transcription, individual nucleotides that are complementary to the ones in the DNA link are sequentially converted into a chain. During translation, amino acids are brought to the mRNA molecule by a transfer RNA (tRNA). The tRNA binds to the mRNA molecule at one end; at the other, it carries a specific amino acid. After its amino acid has joined the growing protein chain, the tRNA moves away.

THE TRANSFORMED CELL

If we consider that an estimated 10^{16} cell divisions take place in a human body over the course of a lifetime and that mutations (the change of one of four bases in the sequence of the DNA) occur spontaneously about every 10^{-6} mutations per gene per cell division, then, in a lifetime, every single gene is likely to have had a mutation 10^{10} different times.[14] This means that the probability for a mutation to occur in genes that regulate cell division is quite high. In fact, if a single mutation were responsible for turning any cell into a malignant one, the chances of cancer in any human being would be so high that we would not be able to live. Luckily for us, cells have mechanisms to repair DNA. They also have several regulatory mechanisms that keep a tight and precise control over their behavior. Because of this, many different regulatory systems have to fail before a cell

GENETIC CAUSES OF CANCER

Scientists believe cancer is caused by the accumulation of several independent mutations in different genes in a single line of cells. Epidemiological studies of the incidence of cancer in relation to age support this theory. If a single mutation were responsible for cancer, the chance of developing cancer would be the same every single year in a person's life. But this is not the case. Data accumulated during many years show that the incidence of cancer rises steeply with age.

This theory of independent, successive mutations as the cause of cancer also provides an explanation for clinical observations of tumor progression in cancer patients. Over time, tumors progress from an initial mild disorder of cell behavior to a full-blown cancer. The incremental progression of tumors provides insight into the molecular nature of the mutations that must occur for the transformation of a normal cell into a cancer cell.

becomes malignant. In other words, cancer is caused not by a single mutation but by a slow accumulation of many random mutations in a single line of cells.[15]

Besides **point mutations** (changes of a single base in the sequence of the DNA molecule), other changes in the DNA sequence that could lead to the transformation of a cell into a cancer include: 1) the deletion of one or more nucleotides from the DNA sequence; 2) the movement of a whole chromosome segment to another chromosome (translocation), or 3) the exchange of segments between two chromosomes.

The exact number of mutations that lead a normal cell to become malignant and the order in which they occur will be different for every cancer cell. Yet there are several steps every cell takes during its progression from normal to cancerous.

Researchers at the Whitehead Institute for Biomedical Research in Cambridge, Massachusetts, have compared the changes that occur in the **genome** of the precancerous cell to the malfunctions that lead to a runaway car: a stuck accelerator, defective brakes, and a gas tank that is always full.[17]

THE STUCK ACCELERATOR: GENES THAT STIMULATE CELL DIVISION BEING PERPETUALLY EXPRESSED

In most cells, cell division occurs in a repeating series of stages called the cell cycle. Cytoplasmic growth takes place during interphase, the stage that comes before cell division. Near the end of the interphase, the DNA replicates and produces two identical copies that then divide into two genetically equivalent nuclei. Division of the **cytoplasm** encloses the nuclei in two separate daughter cells.[18]

Cell division in a multicellular organism is coordinated through factors such as growth factors, or **hormones** that bind to a receptor in the cell membrane. This union sends a signal into the cytoplasm that starts a cascade of reactions ultimately leading to cell division.[19]

Mutations in the genes that encode the components of this signaling (oncogenes) result in a constant signal to divide, even in the absence of the usual hormone. Oncogenes have normal counterparts called **proto-oncogenes**. About 60 different oncogenes have been identified so far. Among those linked to lung cancer are ras, myc, and HER-2/neu.[20]

DEFECTIVE BRAKES: WHEN TUMOR SUPPRESSOR GENES DO NOT FUNCTION PROPERLY

The normal counterparts of the **tumor suppressor genes**— the genes that halt cell division—inhibit tumor growth promoted by oncogenes by encoding proteins that slow or stop cell division. A mutation that eliminates the activity of one of the two copies of the tumor suppressor gene has no effect, because the remaining copy is still active in suppressing cell division. A mutation that eliminates the activity of the second copy of the gene may lead to uncontrolled cell growth. Tumor suppressor genes are thus recessive; both copies have to be mutated to produce this effect.[21] On the other hand, oncogenes are dominant; just a single copy of the oncogene can promote uncontrolled growth.

Some 50 percent of lung cancers have a mutation in the tumor suppressor gene that encodes protein p53. In normal form, p53 combines with and inactivates a variety of proteins that promote cell division—including some that are required for DNA replication—and activates pathways leading to programmed cell death.

Programmed cell death,[22] called **apoptosis** from a Greek word that describes the shedding of leaves, is an important part of normal development and body maintenance. Apoptosis, for example, leads to the loss of the tail in frog embryos and the disappearance of webbing between the fingers and toes in human embryos.

Programmed cell death is ultimately under genetic control. The genes that control cell death are activated by signals

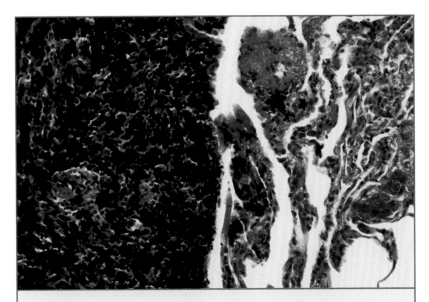

Figure 2.7 This light micrograph of a smoker's lung shows the left side choked with black tar deposits from tobacco smoke. On the right, tar deposits are encroaching on tissue with normal spacing. © Kent Wood/Photo Researchers, Inc.

(hormones and other factors) that arrive at the cell surface as a sort of death notice. Mutations in any of the steps that link the signal to the corresponding gene would cause the cell to fail to kill itself. The survival of and accumulation into masses, or tumors, made of groups of cells that would normally die might lead to cancer.

THE PERPETUALLY FULL GAS TANK

The **telomeres** (*telo* from the Greek meaning *end* and *mere* meaning *segment*) are repetitive sequences that cap the end of each chromosome. Each time the DNA replicates, a piece of telomere is lost. After a certain number of cycles of DNA replications and cell divisions—about 40—the telomere is totally gone, and the cell dies.[23]

During the development of the embryo, when many divisions are necessary, the cells make an enzyme called telomerase that replenishes telomeres. Once the body has reached its full growth, the telomerase gene is turned off. In cancer cells the telomerase gene is expressed, or continues to add the lost segments to the telomeres, and the cell does not die.

In addition to these initial mutations, as a tumor progresses its cells meet new barriers that prevent further growth. For example, when it reaches a size of one or two millimeters in diameter, the cells inside the tumor start to have problems getting the oxygen and nutrients they need to grow. Each time the tumor reaches a new stage, the cells must acquire a specific new mutation that will help them overcome the new barrier. This new mutation may give the cell the ability to make new blood vessels, to invade the surrounding tissues, or to metastasize (spread) to other parts of the body. Another set of mutations in the DNA repair mechanism allows for a higher rate of mutations in a particular cell.

It is not just one genetic defect but a combination of several that allows cancer to develop. These genetic defects can sometimes occur randomly for no apparent reason or sometimes they are inherited, most often they result from exposure to **carcinogens** (cancer-causing chemicals), radiation, or viruses.[24]

Tobacco smoke contains at least 55 known carcinogens, 20 of which have been linked to lung cancer. In fact, smoking accounts for about 90 percent of all cases of lung cancer in humans.[25]

3

What Causes Lung Cancer?

GENETIC CHANGES IN THE DNA

Scientists believe that genetic changes in the DNA of the somatic cells underlie the vast majority of cancers. The following observations support their conclusion.[26]

First, all the cancerous cells in a patient have the same abnormalities in their chromosomes and mutations in their DNA sequence. These are abnormalities that normal cells of the same person do not have.

Second, many of the agents that cause cancer also cause genetic changes. So it seems that **carcinogenesis** (the generation of cancer) is linked with **mutagenesis** (the capability to cause a change in the chromosomal DNA). This is true for chemical carcinogens (which cause point mutations in the DNA), ionizing radiations such as x-rays (which cause chromosome translocation), and viruses (which introduce foreign DNA into the DNA sequence).

Finally, in a significant proportion of people who inherit a strong tendency toward developing cancer, this susceptibility is linked to a genetic defect in the DNA repair mechanism in their cells. When the DNA repair mechanism is defective, the cells cannot fix the mutations that happen routinely as DNA is duplicated. As a result, the mutations occur at a higher rate in these people than in the general population, increasing the possibility for a cancerous cell to develop.

PERSONAL VULNERABILITY

The risk of developing cancer has two main components: our exposure to carcinogens and our personal vulnerability, which in the case of lung cancer includes our genetic heritage and our respiratory health history.

It is widely accepted today that smoking increases the risk of developing lung cancer. Yet not everyone who smokes will get lung cancer, because the genetic heritage of each person is different. Vulnerablility to lung cancer in specific groups of patients—such as those who develop the disease at an early age or nonsmoking women with adenocarcinoma (a type of lung cancer)—seems to run in families. In other words, if your

THE DARK TRUTH ABOUT LIGHT CIGARETTES

Light cigarettes have less tar and nicotine than normal cigarettes. They also have pinpoint holes in their wrappers to let air in and dilute the smoke. Light cigarettes are supposed to lower the risk of lung cancer and other diseases related to smoking by decreasing the amount of the carcinogen components that get into the lungs. When they were tested in machines, they seemed to do so. But in real life their effect is minimal. This is because, unlike the machines used in the testing, real people cover the tiny holes with their lips or fingers when they smoke, minimizing their possible positive effect. As for a lower nicotine content, smokers often compensate for this by taking deeper puffs or by smoking more cigarettes. Some experts believe that taking deeper puffs is the cause of the recent rise in adenocarcinoma, the form of lung cancer that affects smaller airways and the alveoli. Before light cigarettes became available, small cell and squamous cell lung cancer—which affect the larger airways—were the more common types of lung cancer.

Source: Henschke, Claudia I., and Peggy McCarty, with Sarah Wernick. *Lung Cancer: Myths, Facts, Choices—and Hope*. New York: W. W. Norton & Company, 2002.

parents or siblings have had lung cancer, you are at a higher risk to develop the disease.[27]

Lung cancer survivors are at a higher risk than other people for developing a recurrence of lung cancer. Having other lung diseases or poor pulmonary function also increases the risk of lung cancer. Like cancer, chronic bronchitis and emphysema are caused by pollution or smoking. Because they develop faster than cancer, these conditions are a warning sign that cancerous cells may be growing in the lungs. Tuberculosis increases the risk of lung cancer because it may scar the lungs and allow cancer cells to develop in the scarred areas.

PREVENTABLE CAUSES

We cannot change our genetic background or our previous medical history, but we can reduce our risk of developing cancer by limiting our exposure to carcinogens. The carcinogens most clearly linked to lung cancer are radiation (radon and x-rays), asbestos, and many of the chemicals released into the lungs by smoking tobacco or other plants. It is important to avoid carcinogens as much as possible, because they have a synergistic effect: Their effects don't merely add up; they multiply.

Radon and Other Forms of Radiation

Both radon and x-rays are ionizing radiation. They knock electrons out of the atoms that make up molecules and turn them into reactive groups, or ions. This can cause breaks, translocations, or mutations in the DNA, or it can chemically alter molecules such as RNA and proteins. These changes may promote the expression of genes related to cell division or modify controls that regulate the cell cycle. They may also lead to metastasis and the loss of mature cell structure (which would make the cell lose its differentiation). One characteristic of radiation-induced cancer is the long delay—up to 30 to 40 years in some cases—between exposure to the radiation and the development of cancer.

Radon is a colorless, odorless radioactive gas that is found in soil. The connection between lung cancer and radon was made in the 1930s in Czechoslovakian miners. Radon that had accumulated in the mines caused a high rate of lung cancer among miners in a time when lung cancer was almost nonexistent in the rest of the population.

But miners are not the only people at risk. You can be at risk, too. Radon can move from the soil into a building and accumulate in poorly ventilated rooms. According to the Environmental Protection Agency (EPA), one house out of every 15 has elevated radon levels.

Testing for radon is easy: You can buy a radon test kit in a hardware store. If the test is positive, the radon level should be reduced. Sealing foundation cracks and installing a vent pipe system are the most commonly used methods to reduce radon.

Once it gets into the lungs, the radiation from radon can damage lung cells and allow cancer to form. Data from the EPA say that radon contributes to 10,000 lung cancer deaths each year.[28]

X-rays are a valuable tool for diagnosing injuries and certain illnesses. They are also used in the treatment of cancer. In many cases, the benefits of using x-rays outweigh the risks, but x-rays may cause cancer and should be avoided whenever possible.

Several studies have found an elevated incidence of lung cancer in breast cancer survivors who had received radiation treatment years ago, but the treatment techniques used today have greatly reduced unwanted radiation exposure, and the risk for patients is now much lower.

Asbestos

Asbestos is a naturally occurring mineral whose fibers can be woven into lightweight, fire-resistant, and extremely strong materials. Because of these properties, asbestos was used for insulation in homes and office buildings until 1989, when it

Figure 3.1 A specimen of asbestos, the name given to fibrous varieties of distinct mineral species. © Astrid & Hanns-Frieder Michler/Photo Researchers, Inc.

was banned by the EPA because of its cancer-causing effects.[29] Asbestos was also used in shipbuilding and automotive brake repairs.

If asbestos is in good condition, it poses no risk. But asbestos fibers break easily into particles that can float in the air and stick to clothes. If the particles are inhaled, they lodge in the lungs, damaging cells and possibly triggering the development of cancer. The effects of asbestos in the lungs are seen only decades after exposure.

Some people are exposed to asbestos at work—for instance, people who work in asbestos mining and manufacturing or with products that contain asbestos such as brakes or insulation. Among these workers, the risk of lung cancer is 10

3.2 Some Common Chemical Carcinogens and Their Sources

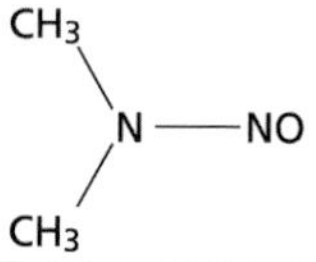

$$\begin{array}{c} CH_3 \\ | \\ N-NO \\ | \\ CH_3 \end{array}$$

dimethylnitrosamine
(leather tanning, beer, herbicides,
tire manufacturing)

$$Br-CH_2-CH_2-Br$$

ethyline dibromide
(fumigant, antiknock
compound in gasoline)

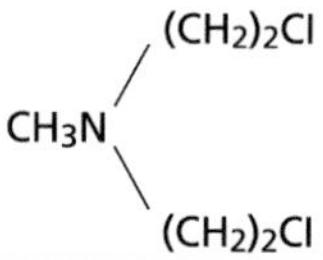

$$\begin{array}{c} (CH_2)_2Cl \\ / \\ CH_3N \\ \backslash \\ (CH_2)_2Cl \end{array}$$

nitrogen mustard
(mustard gas)

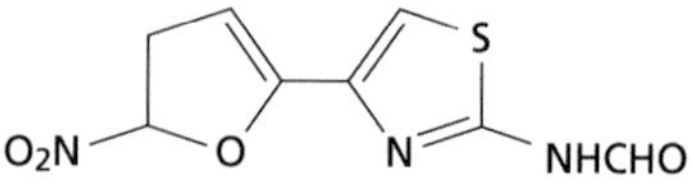

O_2N ⸺ N ⸺ S ⸺ NHCHO

nitrofurans
(human and veterinary medicines,
food preservatives)

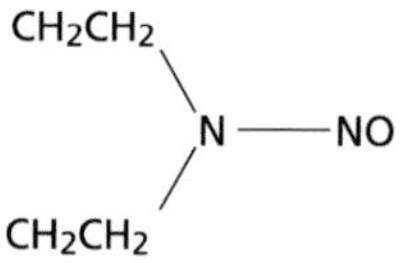

$$\begin{array}{c} CH_2CH_2 \\ \backslash \\ N-NO \\ / \\ CH_2CH_2 \end{array}$$

diethylnitrosamine
(whiskey, new car interiors,
iron foundries)

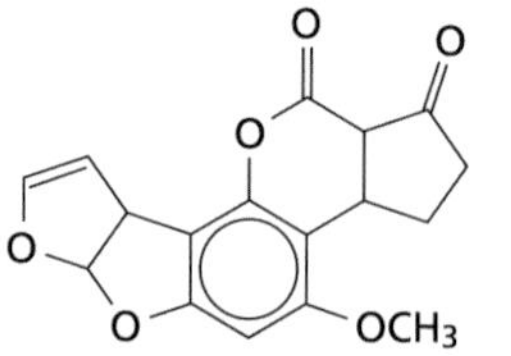

aflatoxin
(fungal product; contaminant in
stored cereal grains,
peanut butter)

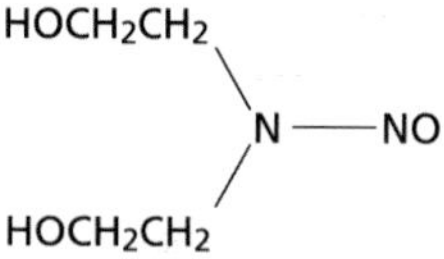

$$\begin{array}{c} HOCH_2CH_2 \\ \backslash \\ N-NO \\ / \\ HOCH_2CH_2 \end{array}$$

N-nitrosodiethanolamine
(cosmetics, lotions, shampoos)

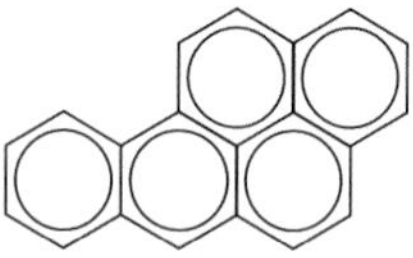

polycyclic hydrocarbons
(wood, coal, cigarette smoke)

times higher for nonsmokers and 90 times higher for smokers[30] when compared with the overall nonsmoking population.

CHEMICAL CARCINOGENS

Most chemical carcinogens (Figure 3.2) belong to three groups: alkylating agents (which substitute a monovalent organic group such as a methyl or ethyl group for a hydrogen atom), polycyclic hydrocarbons, and phorbol esters. Both alkylating agents and polycyclic hydrocarbons are tumor initiators because they can cause mutations. Phorbol esters, on the other hand, are tumor promoters; they do not cause mutations but further the growth of cancer cells.[31]

Many polycyclic hydrocarbons are not carcinogenic in their natural form. They are transformed inside cells into cancer-causing derivatives by a biochemical process called detoxification. Usually detoxification converts substances that are poisonous to the cell into soluble, nontoxic substances that can be excreted. In the case of the polycyclic hydrocarbons, however, it is the soluble form that is highly reactive, causing mutations in the cell DNA and, eventually, cancer.

Polycyclic hydrocarbons are the primary carcinogens found in tobacco and in other smoking products made by the incomplete combustion of organic substances (tobacco or other plant leaves) or fossil fuels (coal or petrol).

Tobacco and Other Kinds of Smoking

What we call tobacco is the dried leaf of the plant *Nicotiana tabacum*. Tobacco leaves are usually rolled (in cigars) or shredded (in cigarettes) and then burned. The smoke is inhaled, allowing its many chemical components to cross the thin-walled alveoli in the lungs and enter the bloodstream.

There are more than 6,800 different chemicals in tobacco smoke,[32] at least 55 of which are known carcinogens. Twenty of these—including benzopyrene, chromium, N-nitrosamine, cadmium, nickel, and arsenic—have been linked to lung cancer.[33]

Smoking is also linked to other cancers, such as cancer of the mouth, throat, esophagus, larynx, pancreas, bladder, kidney, and cervix, as well as metastases from other cancers. It is related to other diseases such as emphysema, heart and circulatory problems—the incidence of heart disease is triple for smokers—and birth defects.[34]

Scientists believe that nicotine, the major psychoactive product in tobacco, is also carcinogenic.[35] Besides this long-term effect, nicotine, when taken in large doses, can cause cramps, vomiting, diarrhea, dizziness, confusion, and trembling. In extreme cases, it can lead to respiratory failure and death.

Most smokers smoke cigarettes. However, smoking cigars or a pipe may cause lung cancer as well. After all, the smoke from cigars and pipes has the same carcinogenic compounds found in cigarette smoke. The reason that the rate of lung cancer is lower among cigar and pipe smokers is that people who smoke this way usually light up less frequently and are less likely to inhale or inhale as deeply as cigarette smokers do.

Smoking other dried plants besides tobacco also carries a significant risk of developing lung cancer and other diseases.[36] For instance, smoking marijuana (*Cannabis sativa*, a kind of Indian hemp)[37] cigarettes causes the same kind of damage to the lungs that smoking tobacco causes. Marijuana cigarettes have more tar than tobacco cigarettes and are not filtered. Besides, although marijuana smokers tend to smoke fewer cigarettes, they inhale more deeply and tend to hold the smoke longer in their lungs.

Smoking exotic flavored cigarettes like bidis and kreteks is also addictive, and poses the same kind of health risks as tobacco cigarettes. Bidis are especially dangerous, because they are not filtered and because they are not packed as tightly as regular cigarettes. This leads smokers to puff harder and more frequently to get the smoke deep into their lungs.

Some of the herbal cigarettes found in health food stores contain tobacco. But even if they don't contain tobacco, they

Figure 3.3 A Local District Conservationist confers with a tobacco farmer in North Carolina. © Photo by Bob Nichols, USDA Natural Resources Conservation Service

have similar levels of tar and other components. When smoked, these will irritate the lungs. Although their health risks, including their link to lung cancer, have not been studied extensively, the risks are presumed to be high.

AVOIDING LUNG CANCER

Considering the low survival rate for lung cancer patients—the two-year survival rate is 20 percent for people with **stage** III disease and only 5 percent for those with stage IV[38]—the best defense against this deadly disease seems to be to avoid exposure to the carcinogens that cause it.

Reduction of asbestos or radon exposure at work and at home could significantly reduce the number of deaths due to lung cancer. Quitting smoking can help even more. According to experts, the elimination of cigarette smoking alone would reduce not only lung cancer, but the total number of deaths from all types of cancer by at least one-third among American and Western European populations.[39]

Despite these overwhelming figures, however, many people seem unwilling or unable to quit smoking until cancer has already developed. By then, it may be too late.

4

Tobacco Smoking and Lung Cancer

STATISTICS ON CIGARETTE SMOKING AND LUNG CANCER

According to the American Cancer Society, cigarette smoking is the leading cause of lung cancer in the United States, accounting for about 87 percent of all the cases. Each year between 1995 and 1999, an average of 124,813 Americans (80,571 men and 44,242 women) died of lung cancer that could be attributed to smoking.[40]

The statistics linking smoking and lung cancer are overwhelming:

- As of 2005 in the United States an estimated 347,000 people had lung cancer, and about 170,000 new cases are diagnosed every year.[41] At the beginning of the twentieth century when the incidence of smoking was lower, lung cancer was a rare disease.

- The rises and declines in the incidence and mortality rates of lung cancer parallel trends of cigarette smoking. The increase in cigarette smoking by men in the 1920s—probably related to an increase in contemporary cigarette production, advertisements, and marketing—was followed in the 1940s by a dramatic increase in the incidence of lung cancer in men.[42] Until the 1960s, lung cancer was rare in women, reflecting the fact that before the 1940s most smokers were men. The number of women smoking increased during the 1940s. Twenty years later, the number of women with lung cancer exploded. Over the next three decades, deaths related to lung cancer in women more than quadrupled. By 1987, for the first time, deaths from lung cancer in women surpassed those from breast cancer.[43]

- The risk of developing lung cancer is 20 times higher for smokers than for nonsmokers. The risk follows the smoking history of the individual, including the length of time the person has smoked and the number of cigarettes he or she smoked per day. The smoking history is measured in pack-years; a pack-year is the equivalent of smoking one pack of cigarettes per day for a year. Table 4.1 shows an example of how to estimate the number of pack-years. The number of pack-years is not the only factor to take into consideration when estimating the risk of lung cancer. The smoking behavior of the individual is also important. Whether the smoker inhales deeply and whether he or she smokes the cigarette completely affects his or her chance of developing lung cancer.

- Smoking-attributable lung cancer death rates per year in the United States range from a high in Kentucky of 121.4 cases per 10,000 people to a low in Utah of 38.7 per 10,000. Smoking prevalence rates are highest in Kentucky and lowest in Utah.[44]

Even if you don't smoke, you may be at risk of developing lung cancer if you spend time with people who do as a result of passive inhalation of both the smoke that the smoker exhales (mainstream smoke) and the smoke from the burning end of the cigarette (sidestream smoke). According to the EPA about 3,000 nonsmokers each year develop lung cancer because they are exposed to secondhand smoke at home or at work.[45]

Today experts agree that smoking causes lung cancer. But the link between smoking and cancer was not always accepted. In fact, the prevailing view in the 1940s was that lung cancer was caused by air pollution, especially the kind created by heavy industry during World War II (1939–1945). For people then, smoking was an everyday activity that everyone did,

Smoking History	Packs	Years	Pack-Years
Moderate smoking in high school, about 10 cigarettes per day	1/2	4	2
Increased smoking for 6 years	1 1/2	6	9
Heavy smoking for 3 years during a period of high stress	2	3	6
Reduced smoking in an effort to quit, before giving up cigarettes completely	1/4	2	1/2
Total Years Smoking		**15**	
Total Pack-Years			**17 1/2**

including glamorous movie stars and increasing numbers of women. It was a habit that went way back to the time before Europeans arrived on the American continent.

SMOKING AND LUNG CANCER: A HISTORY

Centuries before Christopher Columbus landed in North America, Native Americans smoked the shredded, dried leaves of the tobacco plant in wooden or clay pipes. In 1492, members of Christopher Columbus's crew brought the custom back to their native Spain. Later the English settlers did the same. By the seventeenth century, tobacco was the first cash crop in Great Britain's colonies in North America.

At first, smokers followed the Native Americans' custom of burning tobacco in pipes or rolling the leaves into a cigar. Later beggars in Spain collected the cigar butts, transferred the unburnt tobacco into a piece of paper, and wrapped it tightly into what they called cigarettes. Tobacco companies copied the

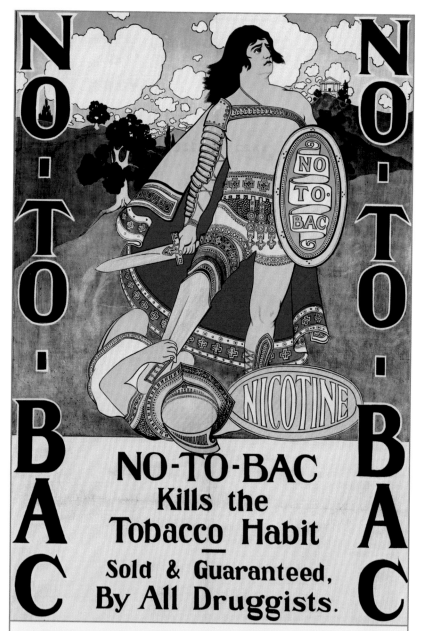

Figure 4.1 Poster painted by Maxfield Parrish to advertise a smoking cessation product, No-To-Bac, 1896. © The Philadelphia Museum of Art/Art Resource, NY

invention and were soon making cigarettes from the leaves left over after cigar production.

Until the 1870s smoking was an expensive habit. The average American smoker only lit up about 40 cigarettes a year. In 1881 the cigarette-rolling machine was invented and cigarettes became more readily available. By 1889 more than 73 billion cigarettes were being produced in the United States,[46] and the consumption of cigarettes increased along with production.

Praised for their relaxation-inducing properties, cigarettes were given to soldiers for free during World War I (1914–1918) and World War II. Hundreds of thousands of nonsmokers were introduced to the habit this way, and continued smoking after returning home from war.

During the 1930s the number of cases of lung cancer—a rare disease until then—started to increase. In 1932 an article published in the *American Journal of Cancer* suggested that tar, a chemical found in tobacco leaves, might be the cause for the rise in lung cancer. But this and other evidence was ignored. Even in 1949, when Ernst Wynder, a medical student at Washington University in St. Louis, Missouri, presented his initial controlled statistical studies that showed a much higher rate of smoking among lung cancer patients than in controls (healthy subjects tested to compare against cancer patients as symptom-free controls), his colleagues were skeptical.

As the then leading thoracic surgeon at Washington University in St. Louis Evarts Graham pointed out: If smoking were connected to lung cancer, then tumors would appear in both lungs—after all, the smoke enters both lungs when you smoke. But, in his experience, lung cancer was usually only present in one lung or the other. Moreover, he also saw lung cancer in patients who had stopped smoking six, eight, or ten years earlier. How could a chemical cause a disease a decade after entering the body? And finally, how could Wynder's theory explain the cases Graham had seen of lung cancer in people who had never smoked?

Wynder could not answer these questions. Yet he continued to collect data on lung cancer patients and smoking. His results, published in 1950 in the *Journal of the American Medical Association* (*JAMA*), were dramatic: Lung cancer risk was in direct proportion to the number of cigarettes smoked, and was as much as 40 times higher for heavy smokers than for nonsmokers. Six months later British epidemiologist Richard Doll published a similar study.[47] The case against smoking was made.

In 1959 U.S. Surgeon General Leroy E. Burney published an article in *JAMA* that said cigarette smoking caused cancer. In 1964 Surgeon General Luther Terry's report on *Smoking and Tobacco* stated, "The risk of developing lung cancer increases with the duration of smoking and the number of cigarettes smoked per day and is diminished by discontinuing smoking."[48]

Although the tobacco industry disputed Terry's findings, in 1966 the federal government ordered that every cigarette pack must carry a warning: "Caution—Cigarette Smoking May Be Hazardous to Your Health."

At the insistence of some scientists who didn't think this warning was strong enough, in 1978 Congress changed the Surgeon General's warning to read: "Smoking Is Known to Cause Cancer and Other Diseases."[49] Despite this and other warnings, 50 million Americans still smoke today.

Some people have believed that the data linking lung cancer and tobacco are circumstantial. Horace R. Kornegay, a former president of the Tobacco Institute, has argued that "the production with smoke of human-type lung cancer—or heart disease or emphysema—has never been verified in laboratory experiments."[50] But most people do not question the link between smoking and lung cancer; they just ignore the risk and convince themselves that they will beat the odds. Or maybe they have tried to quit and failed because smoking, besides being dangerous to the health, is extremely addictive.

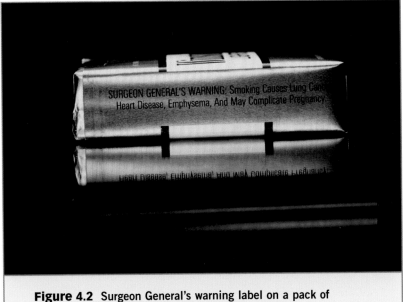

Figure 4.2 Surgeon General's warning label on a pack of cigarettes. © Bill Branson/National Cancer Institute

NICOTINE AND ADDICTION

Cigarette smoking is physically and psychologically addictive because tobacco contains nicotine, and nicotine is as addictive as heroin and cocaine, according to the 1988 U.S. Surgeon General's report.

The nicotine that enters the alveoli after the inhalation of cigarette smoke is absorbed into the bloodstream and reaches the brain in about seven seconds, twice as fast as a shot of heroin injected directly into the vein. As a 1991 editorial in the medical journal *Lancet* put it: "As a drug delivery system the modern cigarette is a highly efficient device for getting nicotine to the brain."[51]

Once in the brain nicotine, like heroin and cocaine, stimulates the reward circuit—the part of the brain that controls feelings of pleasure and well-being. Over time, smokers become accustomed to the emotional effects of nicotine. Cigarettes calm them down, perk them up, and help them focus.

Tobacco companies know this well. Back in the 1960s, the chief counsel of the tobacco company Brown & Williamson wrote in an internal memo, "We are in the business of selling

WAYS TO QUIT SMOKING

Because nicotine is addictive, quitting smoking can be difficult. Nicotine can raise blood pressure, speed up the heartbeat, and cause heartbeat irregularities. This is why it is important to gradually decrease the daily dose of the nicotine replacement until none is needed. Usually, this process takes about 10 weeks. Nicotine replacement products and the drug bupropion are two medical treatments available today that may help people trying to quit.

Nicotine replacement products work by providing alternate sources of nicotine to ease withdrawal symptoms without the health hazards from continued smoking. Nicotine replacements are available as patches, gum, nasal spray, and inhalers. Lollipops may soon be available too. Bupropion (sold under the brand names Amfebutamone®, Wellbutrin®, and Zyban®) is a non-nicotine medication that eases the withdrawal symptoms of nicotine. Bupropion mimics some of the effects of nicotine on the brain.

New approaches for quitting smoking may soon become available. Among those presently being studied are

- a nicotine-blocking vaccine that will keep nicotine from entering the brain;

- an antismoking mouthwash that will make the cigarette smoke taste bad; and

- methoxsalen, a drug that blocks one of the enzymes that metabolizes nicotine in the body. The craving for nicotine

nicotine, an addictive drug effective in the release of stress mechanism."[52]

And in 1972 William L. Dunn, Jr., a senior scientist with the Philip Morris Tobacco Company, wrote, "The cigarette should be conceived not as a product but as a package. The

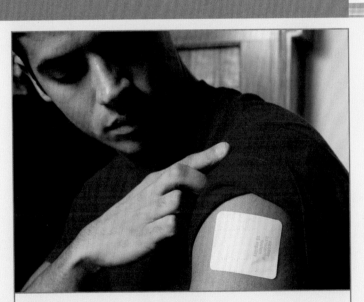

Figure 4.3 Man wearing a nicotine patch. © Doug Martin/ Photo Researchers, Inc.

occurs when blood levels of nicotine fall. By blocking nicotine metabolism, levels of nicotine will remain high and the smoker will not have the craving or the need to smoke.

Source: Henschke, Claudia I., and Peggy McCarty, with Sarah Wernick. *Lung Cancer: Myths, Facts, Choices—and Hope*. New York: W. W. Norton & Company, 2002.

product is nicotine. . . . Think of the cigarette as a dispenser for a dose unit of nicotine…. Think of a puff of smoke as the vehicle of nicotine. Smoke is beyond question the most optimized vehicle of nicotine and the cigarette the most optimized dispenser of smoke."[53]

By 1983, five years before the U.S. Surgeon General's report on nicotine and addiction, researchers for Philip Morris had found that nicotine was addictive in laboratory rats. The results were not widely distributed. Although tobacco companies insisted that nicotine is a natural component in tobacco leaves and that they only used it in cigarettes as a flavor, evidence assembled in a report by FDA investigators in 1994 contradicted the assertion. Tobacco companies had the capability to remove all or almost all of the nicotine from their products. In fact, tobacco companies were already removing nicotine from tobacco leaves, manipulating it, and then adding it back into their final product. If the nicotine collected this way was not high enough to reach their standards, they purchased more nicotine from other sources and added it.[54]

Because nicotine is addictive, quitting smoking is not easy. Stopping the nicotine supply to the brain can cause withdrawal symptoms like cravings, depression, and weight gain. However, some experts like Richard J. DeGrandpre, believe there is more to cigarette addiction than nicotine.

If nicotine were the only reason cigarette smoking is addictive, he argues, nicotine replacement therapies, like the patch, should always work. But the truth is that many people continue to smoke while using the patch, which suggests that the urge to smoke comes from cues other than just low nicotine levels in the blood.

Moreover, if the failure to quit were due only to a physical dependency on nicotine, then relapse would always occur during the two first weeks after quitting, while the withdrawal symptoms were still being experienced. In reality, ex-smokers crave cigarettes at certain times and in certain situations for months, and even years, after quitting.

Addiction to cigarette smoking, DeGrandpre[55] concludes, goes beyond physical addiction to nicotine. Smoking cigarettes, like drinking alcohol, serves as a social lubricant, a method of interaction with other people, and it is triggered by environmental cues, not solely by withdrawal symptoms. Because people smoke in a wide variety of circumstances—when they are bored, after eating, while they are driving—and in different settings—at home, at work, in bars, in the car—the cues to smoke are everywhere, which makes quitting smoking very difficult. (Note: More study of recent legal prohibitions in some U.S. cities against smoking in public restaurants, bars, and workplaces is needed to determine if they affect the overall smoking rate.)

If these cues were not enough to remind smokers about their habit, advertisements might: Cigarettes are the most heavily advertised product in the United States. In 2002 tobacco companies spent more than $34 million per day on the advertising and promotion of their products.[56]

Tobacco companies insist their ads are only intended to attract smokers of other brands of cigarettes to their own. However, many antismoking groups have argued that tobacco advertisement campaigns are responsible for promoting smoking among nonsmokers, especially among the most susceptible part of the population: teenagers and children.

TEENS AND SMOKING

Tobacco kills more people in the United States each year than illegal drugs, homicides, AIDS, car accidents, and alcohol combined.[57] Yet despite the risk, 3,000 teenagers light their first cigarette every day.[58]

Knowing that smoking may lead them to have a heart attack or lung cancer a long time into the future does not seem to deter teens from smoking. But their parents' example might.

Studies show that children of parents who smoke but disapprove of their children's smoking are more likely to smoke than the children of nonsmoking parents who are indifferent to their children's smoking. It seems that it is what the parents *do*, not what they say, that influences their children.

Because children want to be like their parents, smoking for teenagers in many families and communities, is a conformist behavior and a mark of adulthood.[59] For others, however, smoking is an act of rebellion, a protest against authority figures, and a symbol of independence.

It is mainly this last section of the teenage population that the tobacco companies are courting with their advertisements. Tobacco companies present smoking as desirable, glamorous, cool, safe, and healthy. The ads play to teens' desire to be accepted by implying that smoking will improve their self-image and self-confidence, and bring them popularity and the admiration of their peers.

In an effort to prevent smoking, especially among teens, several lawsuits were brought against the tobacco industry during the 1990s. In 1997, several tobacco companies were found guilty of illegally targeting teen smokers through their ad campaigns and the whole tobacco industry was declared guilty of knowingly causing smoking-related deaths and illness.

In 1998, the Master Settlement Agreement (MSA) held the four largest tobacco companies liable for $206 billion to be paid to 46 U.S. states over a period of 25 years, to compensate for tobacco-related health costs.

As a result of the MSA, tobacco companies were forbidden to use cartoon characters in their campaigns or to engage in large-scale outdoor advertising, like billboards. According to many antismoking groups, despite these requirements, the tobacco companies still promote smoking to teens and children by sponsoring sporting events and concerts, advertisements in convenience stores and magazines, and through product placements in films that children are legally allowed to see.[60]

The tobacco companies also pledged, in the MSA, to fund a $1.5 billion, five-year antismoking campaign. As a result of this pledge, starting in 1998, the Philip Morris tobacco company ran the "Think. Don't Smoke" campaign, which featured clean-cut-looking young people explaining why they don't smoke. Another tobacco company, Lorillard, came up with the slogan "Tobacco is Whacko If You Are a Teen" for its campaign. Neither campaign was a great success. In fact, a 2002 survey of teenagers showed that the "Think" campaign had the opposite effect: It encouraged teens to smoke.[61]

Since 2000, the American Legacy Foundation, a nonprofit antismoking organization, has been running its own national antismoking campaign, called "Truth." Both in its TV and print commercials, "Truth" features edgy youths delivering stark facts about the tobacco industry's historical denial of tobacco's health effects and of their youth-oriented marketing practices. For example, one commercial shows young people piling body bags in front of a tobacco company's headquarters and explaining through megaphones that the bags represent the 1,200 people killed by smoking every day. By showing youths rebelliously rejecting tobacco and tobacco advertising, the "Truth" commercials channel the teens' need to assert their independence and individuality, while at the same time countering tobacco marketing efforts.

Results from two national surveys demonstrate that the "Truth" campaign has been effective in raising teens' awareness of the dangers of smoking and the subtle ways the tobacco companies push their products on them. These surveys also found a reduction in the intention to smoke among youths at risk.[62] Yet none of the campaigns changed the teens' perception that smoking makes them look cool and helps them fit in with their peers.

Whether they smoke to be like their parents or to be cool and accepted by peers, holding a cigarette is for many teens a symbol of being a grown-up. Telling those teens that smoking is only for adults or demonizing it may only increase its attraction.

Teenage smoking is not as bleak as some have portrayed it, though. Although it is true that 5 million children smoke, 20 million do *not* smoke.[63] These data alone belie one common teenage excuse, "Everybody smokes."

Besides, compared with 30 percent of adults in the 25 to 64 year old range who smoke, only 22 percent of high school seniors do. Of this 22 percent, only 13 percent smoke half a pack of cigarettes or more per day.[64] Statistics show that of those who try cigarettes as teenagers less than one-third will continue to smoke when they are older.[65]

5

Detecting Lung Cancer: Symptoms and Screening

Lung cancer is difficult to discover because it does not have a single pattern of symptoms. As the disease progresses, some people may have symptoms pointing to a problem in the respiratory system such as difficulty breathing or hoarseness, while others complain of headaches, back pain, or swollen fingertips. The most common symptom is fatigue. But fatigue and all of the other symptoms just mentioned may be caused by diseases other than lung cancer.

The reason lung cancer symptoms are so diverse is because they may have three very different causes: the actual tumor growing in the lungs, tumor metastases to other parts of the body, or hormones and other molecules secreted by the lung cancer cells.

SYMPTOMS CAUSED BY TUMOR GROWTH IN THE LUNGS AND CHEST

Symptoms caused directly by tumor growth in the lungs and chest include fatigue or weakness; breathlessness; repeated bouts of pneumonia; coughing; hoarseness; noisy breathing; pain or weakness in the back, chest, shoulders, or arms; difficulty swallowing; swelling of the face and neck; and lumps near the neck. As the tumor grows, it can block an airway and the supply of oxygen in the blood may not be enough, causing fatigue and weakness.

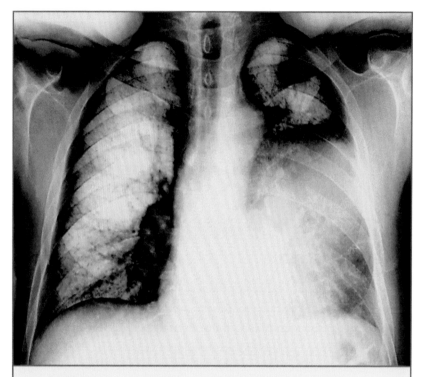

Figure 5.1 Colored x-ray of the chest of a 62-year-old patient with a cancerous lung tumor at upper right. The tumor has blocked the passage (bronchus) into the left lung, causing the collapse of the upper lobe. © Zephyr/Photo Researchers, Inc.

Lung cancers may cause shortness of breath in many ways. The tumor can block a major airway and block the passage of air into an entire lung. The growing of the tumor may cause fluid to collect around the outside of a lung and take up so much space within the chest cavity that the lung cannot fully expand. Lung cancer may affect the sac that surrounds the heart, called the pericardium. The cancer may cause fluid to build up within the sac, preventing the heart from working properly and causing shortness of breath. Finally, if the tumor

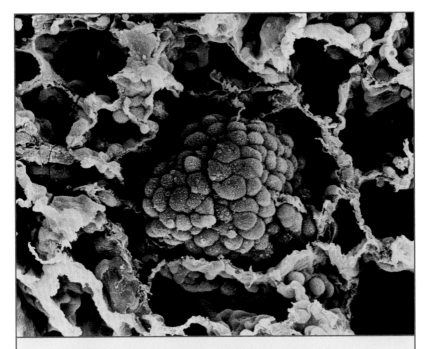

Figure 5.2 Colored scanning electron micrograph of a small cancerous tumor (center) filling an alveolus of the human lung. © Moredun Scientific/Photo Researchers, Inc.

damages one of the nerves that control the diaphragm, part of the diaphragm may become paralyzed. The movement of air in and out of the chest decreases, causing shortness of breath.

When a tumor blocks an airway, it may prevent mucus from moving up and cause the airway to become infected. This may lead to repeated bouts of pneumonia.

Coughing is the body's mechanism for clearing irritants and fluids from its airways. Respiratory infections, asthma, smoking, allergies, and polluted air can trigger coughing. Lung cancer leads to coughing when the tumor is in the central part of the airway or if the cancer produces fluid, but not when the cancer is in the smaller airways and alveoli. When the surface of the tumor bleeds, the mucus excreted with the cough may be tinged with blood. Coughing blood, called hemoptysis, is a serious symptom and should be evaluated immediately.

If the tumor is located near the larynx (voice box) or if it presses on the nerves associated with the larynx, it can cause hoarseness. If it compresses or blocks the esophagus, it can cause dysphagia, or difficulty swallowing.

Swelling of the face and neck may occur when the cancer has invaded the mediastinum (the space between the lungs). This happens when the tumor presses against the superior vena cava, the vein that returns blood to the heart from the head, neck, chest, and arms. Eventually a severe headache, blurring of vision, and even loss of consciousness may occur if the problem is not addressed.

SYMPTOMS CAUSED BY METASTASES BEYOND THE CHEST

Once the lung cancer has metastasized outside the chest, it may cause symptoms that are totally unrelated to the respiratory system. A metastasis to the brain can cause severe headaches, blurred vision, confusion, seizures, or changes in personality or mental functioning. When a cancer spreads to the bones, it may cause an aching pain. The most common sites for bone metastases are in the spine, the pelvic bone, and the femur. Bones that have been invaded by cancer may fracture easily. Back pain can be caused by cancer in the spine or by a tumor pressing on a nerve.

SYMPTOMS CAUSED BY TUMOR SECRETIONS

Some tumors secrete hormones or other substances that can cause symptoms known as paraneoplastic syndromes (*para* from the Greek meaning *along with* and *neoplastic* refers to *neoplasm* for *tumor*). Having these symptoms does not necessarily mean that the cancer has spread; tumor secretions may reach parts of the body where the cancer itself isn't present. The

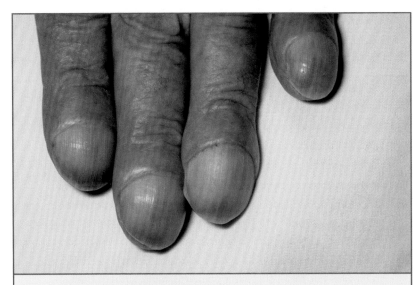

Figure 5.3 Clubbed fingers caused by lung cancer.
© Dr. M.A. Ansary/Photo Researchers, Inc.

most common paraneoplastic syndromes are weight loss—with or without loss of appetite—and changes in the fingertips: the fingers become wider and puffier, and the nails curved as if they were hunchbacked. This is called digital clubbing.

People with cancer sometimes lose weight even if they are eating normally. This condition, called cancer wasting, appears to be triggered by substances that the tumor releases into the bloodstream and by certain responses of the immune system to the cancer.

Other symptoms caused by tumor secretions include mental confusion, muscle weakness (especially in the legs), unsteady balance, water retention, night sweats, and hot flashes.

SCREENING

Because the early symptoms of lung cancer can be so different from one person to the next and can be explained by

other, more common conditions, from pneumonia to insuffi-
cient sleep or lack of exercise, lung cancer usually goes unno-
ticed. By the time the best-known symptom of lung cancer

THE CASE FOR LUNG CANCER SCREENING

A century ago a cancer diagnosis was almost always a death
sentence. But today it does not have to be. According to the
National Cancer Institute, the five-year survival rate varies
according to the type of cancer, from a high of 84 percent for
women diagnosed with breast cancer and 87 percent for men
diagnosed with prostate cancer, to 61 percent for colon cancer and 14 percent for lung cancer. Lung cancer's low survival
rate does not mean that lung cancer is more virulent than
other types of cancer. The reason is that lung cancer is usually found too late for effective treatment.

All cancerous tumors can grow silently for months or years
without producing any obvious symptoms. This is even more
so for lung cancer because the lungs contain no pain termi-
nals to alert the body that something is wrong. Because most
people have a much greater lung capacity than they need to
function normally, a tumor growing inside the bronchi or alveoli doesn't necessarily translate into shortness of breath. By
the time the tumor is large enough to hinder breathing or
cause a cough or pain, it is probably too advanced to cure.

This is why many doctors believe an annual screening for
people at high risk for lung cancer should be implemented.
According to Dr. Betty Flehinger, a medical statistician from
the T. J. Watson Research Center in New York, an annual
screening with standard x-rays might reduce lung cancer mortality by 13 percent. Screening with a CT scan could mean a
cure rate as high as 80 or 90 percent.

Source: Henschke, Claudia I., and Peggy McCarty, with Sarah Wernick.
  Lung Cancer: Myths, Facts, Choices—and Hope. New York: W. W.
  Norton & Company, 2002.

—coughing up blood—appears, the disease is often too advanced to cure.

In those cases where lung cancer is discovered earlier—perhaps by chance when the person happens to have a chest x-ray, CT scan, or **MRI** for another medical condition—before it produces symptoms and before it has spread, the five-year survival rate is about 70 percent.[66]

Even though detecting the cancer in its earlier stages seems to be the key to a better chance of survival, lung cancer screening is controversial. Unlike early detection tests for breast, cervical, colon, prostate, and skin cancer, which are routinely done, lung cancer **screening** is not recommended by any major health organizations, including the American Cancer Society, the National Cancer Institute, and the American Medical Association.

These organizations base their decision on several studies performed in the 1970s. The studies used chest x-rays and sputum cytology to screen for lung cancer in a total of 31,360 male heavy smokers. Sputum cytology is the analysis under a microscope of the cells present in the mucus (sputum) excreted from the lungs and airways. The goal of this technique is to see cancerous lung cells before the lung tumor is big enough to be detected.

The results of these studies were disappointing. The sputum cytology detected some, but not all, of the early cases of lung cancer. Follow-up of these early cases showed no increase in the survival rate. The use of chest x-rays every four months to detect earlier cases of cancer did not increase the chance of survival, either.

Since this study was done, some researchers have reexamined the data of the investigation and found them flawed. For instance, many of the people in the study were not checked as often as planned, and the control group in the x-ray experiment was also examined by x-ray, but the experimental group received the x-ray exam every four months, while the control group received it only once a year. Also, the two groups were too similar to reveal any benefit from the screening.

But even if the data were not flawed, the methods of detection have improved since the 1970s, and many physicians and researchers believe screening for lung cancer in high-risk groups should be done today. Among them, Claudia Henschke and her colleagues at Weill Medical College of Cornell University in New York City have been screening people who are at risk for lung cancer since the early 1990s with encouraging results using an imaging technique called a **CT scan.**

While x-rays take a fixed picture of the lung, the spiral CT scanner takes a series of pictures (300–600 in a single breath-hold) as it moves in a quick, smooth spiral around the patient's body. The scanner feeds these pictures into a computer, which reassemble them into a three-dimensional image of the lungs.

In their first study (1992–1998), Henske and her team were able to detect lung cancer in 27 out of 1,000 high-risk volunteers. None of these people had any symptoms, and only four of these 27 very early cancers were visible on x-rays. The study, published in 1999[67] in *Lancet*, encouraged 20 institutions in the United States to join in a collaborative research effort to develop a screening protocol for lung cancer using CT scans.

Having a CT scan done is only the first step of the screening procedure, though. To have an experienced person interpret the result and a good follow-up system are even more important for a good diagnosis than the sensitivity of the CT scan itself.

In a CT scan, a tumor will look like a white nodule. Not all white areas detected in a CT scan are cancer, however. To avoid false negatives, the nodule must be measured and its shape examined. If it is 11 millimeters (0.4 inches) or larger (bigger than a small lima bean) or if its appearance suggests **malignancy**, a **biopsy** is recommended. If it is smaller, the scan will be repeated in three months to see if it has changed. Then, the proper treatment is implemented.

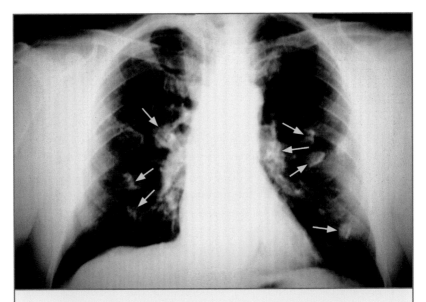

Figure 5.4 A chest x-ray, frontal view, showing malignant tumors. © James Cavallini/Photo Researchers, Inc.

Additional techniques discussed below also hold promise for lung cancer screening.

Chest X-Rays

Although not as sensitive as a CT scan, chest x-rays can detect nodules of about 30 millimeters (a little over an inch) in diameter. With computerized chest x-ray analysis, the resolution increases and lesions as small as 9 millimeters (0.35 inches) become visible.

Sputum Cytology

Several improvements in this technique since the 1970s make it a very valuable tool for the early detection of lung cancer. Improvements include a better method for collecting a sample and the use of techniques that allow the detection of molecular markers (mutations in oncogenes and tumor suppressor genes) in the sputum cells months before there is any other evidence of lung cancer. Also, the use of dyes to highlight abnormal cells and computer-assisted reading can avoid errors in interpretation.

Blood Tests

Although not possible today, researchers are looking for molecules specifically secreted by the transformed cells that could be detected in blood. One promising possibility involves the detection of evidence of damage to the p53 gene. As we saw in chapter 2, damage to the p53 gene (a tumor suppressor gene) has been linked to lung cancer. When the p53 gene is damaged, it produces a defective protein. This abnormal p53 protein triggers the production of p53 antibodies that can be detected in the blood. Unlike people with cancer, healthy individuals rarely have these antibodies.

6

Diagnosis and Staging

The diagnosis of lung cancer is always a multistep process. It starts with a physical examination by a general physician. Then, if cancer is suspected, a specialist will perform additional tests to confirm the **diagnosis**.

PHYSICAL EXAMINATION

As part of the physical examination, the general physician will listen to the patient's chest, check for fluid in the lungs or obstructions in the breathing passages, and conduct pulmonary function tests to check for reduced airflow. Because lung cancer can also affect other parts of the body, the doctor may also check weight and blood pressure, check the eyes for signs of increased pressure from the brain, check for enlarged lymph nodes above the collarbone, look for signs of fluid retention such as swollen ankles, and feel if the liver is enlarged.

The doctor will probably order standard blood and urine tests to eliminate any other possible explanation for the patient's symptoms, such as anemia or infection.

Sputum cytology—the microscopic evaluation of coughed-up material—may be performed to look for cancer cells. Because it is difficult to get a sample from deep inside the lungs, a negative result doesn't always mean there is no cancer.

If the physician suspects lung cancer, he or she will refer the patient to a pulmonologist (a doctor who treats disorders of the lungs and chest) or an oncologist (a cancer specialist). The specialists will order one or more imaging tests to visualize any possible tumor. If a tumor is detected, a biopsy will be done to check whether the cells in the tumor are cancerous and to determine the type of lung cancer.

IMAGING TESTS

Chest X-Ray

A chest x-ray is the most common imaging study performed when a lung disease is suspected. In addition to detecting a tumor, an x-ray image can also detect an abnormal widening of the area between the lungs, which may indicate the presence of a tumor or the presence of lymph nodes that have enlarged as the result of a tumor. An x-ray may also show signs of pneumonia by detecting fluid around the lungs, or even abnormalities in the bones.

Comparisons of earlier x-rays with a recent one will allow the doctor to estimate the growth of a tumor. If it has not grown or changed in the last two years, the chance that a tumor is cancerous is less than 5 percent.

CT Scan

The use of a computerized tomography (CT; also called computerized axial tomography, or CAT) scan provides more detail than an x-ray. It can better identify characteristics of the tumor,

LUNG CANCER AND HEALTH HISTORY

Because the symptoms for lung cancer are not specific and can usually be explained by other common conditions, the disease sometimes goes undetected or is misdiagnosed.

That is why the health history of the individual—age, smoking and family history, and occupational exposure—is particularly important in diagnosing lung cancer and should always be brought to the physician's attention.

For example, shortness of breath and coughing in a 20-year-old person who has never smoked are probably not caused by lung cancer. But if the person is 65 years old and has smoked for the last 40 years, the same symptoms have a higher probability of being the result of lung cancer.

such as calcification or an irregular surface. It is also more accurate at identifying enlarged lymph nodes in the lung or in the center of the chest. Enlarged lymph nodes may contain metastatic lung cancer cells. Sometimes, a dye is injected in the patient to heighten the contrast between different types of tissues.

Positron Emission Tomography (PET) Scan

A **PET** scan is another imaging test. Unlike x-rays and CT scans that detect structures of the body, PET highlights areas where sugar metabolism is high. Because rapidly growing cells—such as cancer cells—take up sugar more quickly than other cells, the areas highlighted by the PET scan could very possibly be cancerous.

Studies have found that PET scans can detect metastases that CT scans and other standard procedures had missed, and can determine the stage of the cancer, avoiding the need for more invasive procedures. To know whether the cancer has spread to other areas is extremely important because if it has, surgery may not be the best treatment option.

New equipment can perform both a CT scan and a PET scan simultaneously, providing the diagnosis and the information about metastases in less than half an hour.

BIOPSY

Imaging techniques reveal the location and other features of a tumor, but it is necessary to perform a **biopsy** to determine with total certainty that the tumor is cancer.

A biopsy is always an invasive procedure. To extract the sample, the physician must get into the lung. Depending on the size and location of the tumor, the physician will choose the most appropriate of the following methods.

Bronchoscopy

A bronchoscope is a long, flexible telescope about the width of a pencil, with a fiberoptic light and a camera at the end.

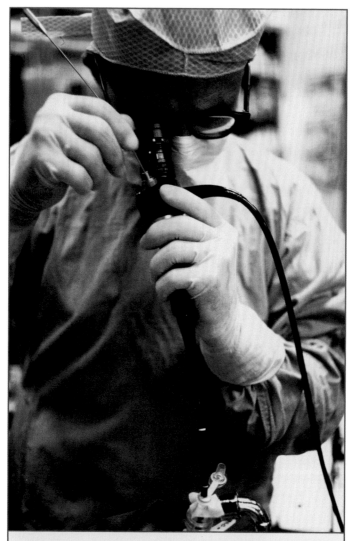

Figure 6.1 A physician inserts a bronchoscope, a flexible tube with a light inside, into a patient's trachea to view inside the body. © National Cancer Institute

During a bronchoscopy, a bronchoscope is snaked through the nose or mouth into the patient's major bronchial tubes. Sometimes, an x-ray is used to help guide the tube. The bronchoscope allows the doctor to see the inside of the bronchi and take samples of tissue and sputum to confirm the presence of lung cancer and determine its type. This test is recommended if an x-ray or CT scan has shown a suspicious tumor in the central part of the lungs. But it is less reliable for examining tumors farther out toward the edges of the lung. In a fluorescent bronchoscopy, the test is performed under a special fluorescent light that shows the tumor more clearly.

A bronchoscopy can take from 30 minutes to several hours. To minimize discomfort, the patient is sedated and given local anesthesia. Medication is needed to control any gagging and coughing, and oxygen is administered to help the patient breathe.

Fine Needle Aspiration

Another way to obtain a tissue sample is to insert a very thin, hollow needle between two ribs into the lung. Using an x-ray or CT scan to locate the suspect area, the surgeon or radiologist performing the operation will suck some of the cells into a syringe attached to the needle. This technique is used mainly to study tumors that are located closer to the chest wall. It can also be used to biopsy enlarged lymph nodes.

This procedure is quite safe, but there is a small chance of life-threatening complications such as bleeding inside the lung or lung collapse. Usually, the collapsed lung reexpands on its own. In some cases, a larger chest tube has to be placed between the ribs to expand the lung.

Another drawback of this technique, especially when the tumor is small, is that the doctor must be highly skilled to diminish the chances that the needle will miss the tumor.

Thoracentesis

Thoracentesis refers to the extraction of fluid with a hollow needle from the space between the lungs and the membranes that surround them (the pleura). The accumulation of fluid in this space (pleural effusion) can compress the lungs and impair breathing. This condition can be caused by an infection or by secretions from lung cancer cells.

Mediastinoscopy

Mediastinoscopy is the insertion of a viewing instrument (a mediastinoscope) through a small incision made at the base of the neck just above the breastbone (the long, flat bone that runs through the center of the chest). The mediastinoscope is inserted along the trachea into the mediastinum, the space between the two lungs, and used to collect a tussue sample. Other instruments inserted through additional incisions allow the doctor to collect tissue samples from tumors or lymph nodes to check for cancer.

Thorascopy

If the lung tumor is near the surface of the lung, a thorascopy can be used to perform an excisional biopsy. To perform a thorascopy, the surgeon makes a small incision between the ribs and inserts a special tube that holds a small television camera. This camera allows the surgeon to view the lining of the chest and the surface of the lungs on a television monitor. Other small incisions are then made to insert surgical instruments that can be used to biopsy lung tumors and lymph nodes that may contain cancer. Unlike the needle biopsy, which takes a sample of the tissue, the excisional biopsy removes the entire tumor. The thorascopy can also be used to remove a complete lobe of a lung, or even the entire lung. Because the incisions are small and the ribs do not have to be spread apart, this is actually a minimally invasive technique.

Both the mediastinoscopy and the thorascopy are performed under total anesthesia.

OTHER TESTS TO DETECT METASTASES

To give a complete diagnosis, tests are also performed to search

6.2 Common Sites for Lung Cancer Metastasis

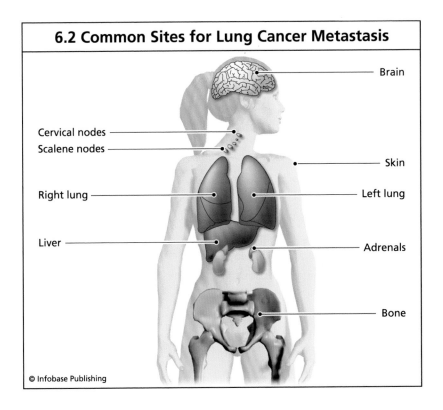

© Infobase Publishing

for metastases. Lung cancer usually spreads to the bones, the brain, the liver, and the adrenal glands (Figure 6.2). The most common tests used are an MRI (magnetic resonance imaging) of the brain and bones, bone scan, and ultrasound scan or CT scan of the adrenal glands, liver, and bones.

Once lung cancer has been confirmed, the next step is to determine what kind of lung cancer it is, what grade, and what stage it has reached. This information is a very important part of the diagnosis because it will guide the choice of treatments.

TYPES OF LUNG CANCER

There are more than a dozen different types of lung cancer, each with its own appearance, typical causes, and patterns of growth. Until more is known about the genetic origin of the lung cancer cells, lung cancers are divided into two main categories based on the size and appearance of the cells: small cell lung cancer (SCLC) and non-small cell lung cancer (NSCLC).

Small Cell Lung Cancer (SCLC)

SCLC is also called oat cell carcinoma because the cells resemble oats under a microscope. It is the type of cancer found in about 20 to 25 percent of people with lung cancer, almost always in smokers.

SCLC usually develops in the secretory cells (neuroendocrine cells) that line the bronchial airways. These cells produce hormones; therefore, SCLC tumors can produce hormones and cause paraneoplastic syndromes.[68] For instance, if the cells produce cortisone, the condition is called Cushing's syndrome; if it produces antidiuretic hormone (ADH), the body will retain water and the apparent salt (sodium) level decreases. Each of these tumors produces its own symptoms.

SCLC is not always confined to the lung. It may occur in the esophagus, prostate, or cervix. Sometimes, its site of origin cannot be determined.

The cells in the SCLC divide rapidly; the **doubling time** for the tumor is only about 30 days. SCLC is a particularly aggressive form of cancer that spreads quickly and usually involves multiple tumors throughout the lung. By the time the diagnosis is made, the cancer may have spread to the lymph nodes in the center of the chest (mediastinal nodes), in the neck and above the collarbone (supraclavicular nodes), and in the abdominal cavity. It may even have spread through the bloodstream, liver, lungs, brain, and bones. In the most common scenario, SCLC presents small primary tumors in the lung and large mediaclonal lymph nodes.

Non-Small Cell Lung Cancer (NSCLC)

NSCLC includes several different forms. Some grow as quickly as the SCLC, but the usual doubling time is 30 to 180

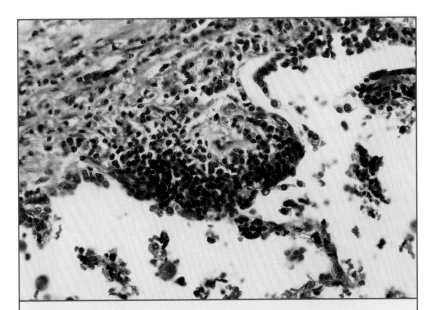

Figure 6.3 Small cell lung cancer, also called oat cell carcinoma. This type of cancer gets its name from its small, densely packed oat-grain-like cells. © Michael Abbey/Photo Researchers, Inc.

days. Because of this, NSCLC is more often confined to the chest at the time of the diagnosis. There are several types of NSCLC.

Adenocarcinoma

Adenocarcinoma begins in the smaller airways and the alveoli. The cancerous cells are tall and cylindrical. Adenocarcinoma strikes nonsmokers most frequently, and in many cases, seems to arise at the site of old scars.

Adenocarcinoma is on the rise among smokers. Many experts believe this is because of the switch to filtered cigarettes. Smokers inhale more deeply when they smoke filtered cigarettes, which allows carcinogens to reach the smaller airways and alveoli, where adenocarcinoma starts. Adenocarcinoma is also increasing among women, who seem to be more

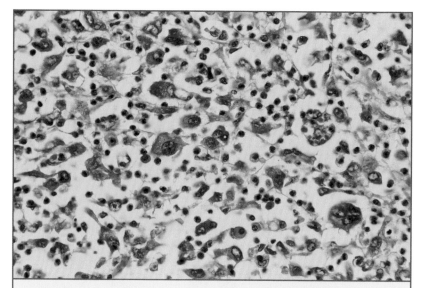

Figure 6.4 Giant cell carcinoma. © Michael Abbey/Photo Researchers, Inc.

susceptible to it than men. Adenocarcinomas make up about 40 percent of all lung cancers.[69]

One distinct type of adenocarcinoma is bronchoalveolar carcinoma, which causes mucus-producing cells to proliferate on the walls of the alveoli. Unlike other adenocarcinomas, it usually involves multiple tumors. It grows slowly, with a dividing time of 180 days or more.

Squamous Carcinoma

Squamous carcinoma, so-called because its cells are thin and flat and resemble fish scales, usually develops in the large bronchial tubes in the center of the lungs. It advances more slowly than the other forms of lung cancer. Squamous carcinoma occurs more frequently in elderly men who smoke or have smoked. Most likely due to changes in smoking patterns, its incidence is decreasing.

Large Cell and Giant Cell Carcinoma

As the names imply, these forms of cancer usually have larger cells than other lung cancers. They usually start in the smaller airways and then grow rapidly. The cause is almost always smoking. Large cell and giant cell carcinomas comprise about 10 percent of all lung cancers. [70]

TUMOR GRADE

As we saw in chapter 1, normal cells are differentiated—they have a distinct appearance that makes them suitable to perform their function. As the tumor grows, its cells become less and less differentiated. The more abnormal the cells appear when examined under the microscope, the more aggressive the cancer is likely to be. Tumor cells are graded on a scale of 1 to 4. The higher numbers indicate a more advanced degree of de-differentiation (abnormality).

STAGING

Staging is the process of determining how far a cancer has spread. Stage I is early cancer: The cancer is found only inside the lung. Stage IV is the most advanced: The lung cancer has metastasized to other parts of the body. Staging is determined by imaging techniques and biopsies. The staging system is universal. It allows researchers from all over the world to communicate and doctors to better devise a treatment plan.

The stage of the disease is the most important indicator of a person's **prognosis**, the likely outcome of the disease. The prognosis of a person with lung cancer is usually expressed as the probability that he or she will be alive five years after the diagnosis.

The staging system is based on three factors: the size and location of the tumor (T), the extent of lymph node involvement (N), and presence or absence of metastases (M). Because SCLC and NSCLC have different patterns of growth, they are staged differently.

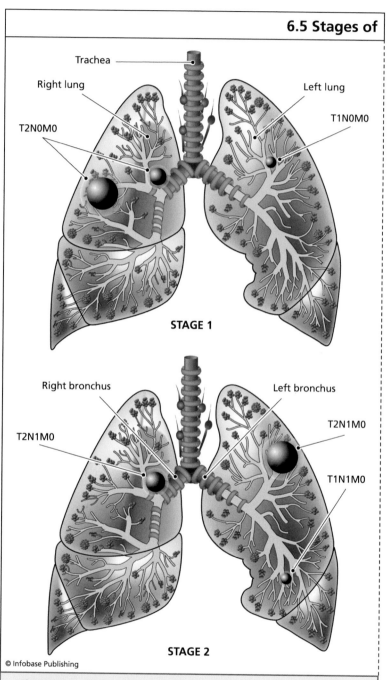

6.5 Stages of

Trachea

Right lung

Left lung

T1N0M0

T2N0M0

STAGE 1

Right bronchus

Left bronchus

T2N1M0

T2N1M0

T1N1M0

STAGE 2

© Infobase Publishing

Figure 6.5 Stages of lung cancer, showing size and location of primary cancer, and lymph nodal involvement.

Lung Cancer

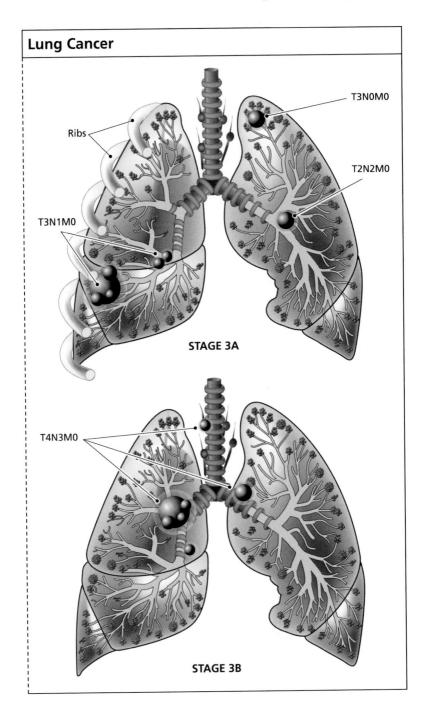

Ribs

T3N0M0

T2N2M0

T3N1M0

STAGE 3A

T4N3M0

STAGE 3B

Table 6.1 Non-Small Cell Lung Cancer: T-N-M Classification

T/Tumor	N/Lymph Nodes	M/Metastases
T0: Cancer cells found in bronchial secretions, but no tumor is visible	**N0:** No lymph node involvement	**M0:** No evidence that cancer has spread to other organs or to lymph nodes outside the chest and neck
T1: Tumor is 3 centimeters or smaller and is completely surrounded by lung tissue	**N1:** Only lymph nodes within the affected lung are involved; this may include the hilar lymph nodes (nodes near the hilum, the point where the lung attaches to the main airway)	**M1:** Cancer has spread to other organs or to lymph nodes outside the chest and neck.
T2: Tumor is larger than 3 centimeters and is completely surrounded by lung tissue	**N2:** Involvement of lymph nodes in the mediastinum (area between the lungs) on the ipsilateral side (same as the tumor)	
T3: Tumor is any size and has invaded the chest wall	**N3:** Involvement of the hilar or mediastinal lymph nodes on the contralateral side (opposite from the tumor)	
T4: Tumor is any size and has invaded vital structures outside the lung or has produced malignant pleural effusion (fluid between the lungs and the chest wall)		

Source: Henschke, Claudia I., Peggy McCarty with Sarah Wernick. *Lung Cancer: Myths, Facts, Choices—and Hope.* New York: W.W. Norton and Company, 2002.

Staging of Non-Small Cell Lung Cancer

The first step in staging NSCLC is to assign a numerical value to T, N, and M according to descriptions seen in Table 6.1. The

Table 6.2 **Stages of Non-Small Cell Lung Cancer**

Stage		T-N-M Description	What It Means
0		T0-N0-M0	Cancer cells have been detected in sputum, but no evidence of cancer has been found on chest x-ray or CT. Some of these very early cancers may be eliminated by the immune system. In the future, we may have chemopreventive treatments— medications that can keep these cancers from advancing further.
I	IA IB	T1-N0-M0 T2-N0-M0	Stage I is very early lung cancer that shows no signs of having spread. Chances of a cure are excellent, particularly if the tumor is one of the smaller ones detected by CT. The usual treatment is surgical removal of the affected lobe of the lung. Radiation therapy is used instead when the patient cannot undergo surgery for medical reasons. Chemoprevention and other new techniques may be helpful as well.
II	IIA IIB	T1-N1-M0 T2-N1-M0 T3-N0-M0	Stage II is early lung cancer that has spread to the chest wall or to lymph nodes within the affected lung (including the hilar lymph nodes), but not beyond. Chances of a cure are very good. The usual treatment is surgery to remove the affected part of the lung and the cancerous nodes; sometimes radiation and chemotherapy are administered as well. Radiation alone may be used if the patient is unable to withstand surgery.
III	IIIA	T3-N1-M0 T1-N2-M0 T2-N2-M0 T3-N2-M0	In stage IIIA, the cancer has spread to the chest wall or mediastinal lymph nodes; it is still confined to the same side as the affected lung. Combinations of surgery, radiation, and chemotherapy offer the best chance for cure or long-term survival. Treatment may begin with surgery; sometimes surgery is delayed until radiation or chemotherapy shrinks the tumor.
	IIIB	T4-N0-M0 T4-N1-M0 T2-N3-M0 T3-N3-M0	In stage IIIB, lung cancer has spread to the opposite side of the chest or is producing malignant pleural effusion. Usually surgery is not recommended. The best hope for long-term survival is a combination of chemotherapy and radiation. Sometimes this treatment shrinks the tumor enough to permit surgery.
IV		M1 with any T and any N	At stage IV, lung cancer has spread outside the chest. Surgery may be possible if both the original tumor in the lung and the metastasized tumor are very small. Though the disease usually is not considered curable at this stage, radiation and chemotherapy—often using combinations of drugs—can do much to extend survival time and improve comfort.

Source: Henschke, Claudia I., Peggy McCarty with Sarah Wernick. *Lung Cancer: Myths, Facts, Choices—and Hope.* New York: W.W. Norton and Company, 2002.

higher the number, the more advanced the disease. For instance, T1-N1-M0 means the tumor is no bigger than 3 centimeters (1.2 inches) and is completely surrounded by lung tissue. Lymph nodes within the lung are involved but there is no sign of metastasis outside the lungs.

In the current system of classification, the smallest tumor is about 3 centimeters. Yet CT scans can now find tumors smaller than 10 millimeters (0.4 inches). Eventually the NSCLC staging will be updated to include improvements made in the detection of very small tumors.

The second step in staging consists of associating the T-N-M description to a particular stage as shown in Table 6.2, where T1-N1-M0 corresponds with Stage II. The chances of cure and suggested treatment(s), depending on the stage of the cancer, are given in Table 6.2.

Staging of Small Cell Lung Cancer(s)

Small cell lung cancers are classified as limited stage or extensive, though the NSCLC classification is beginning to be used. Limited stage SCLC is approximately equivalent to stages I to IIIA of NSCLC (see Table 6.2). It means that the cancer affects one or both lungs and possibly also the mediastinum and lymph nodes in the chest. Extensive SCLC, equivalent to stages IIIB and IV, means that the SLCL has spread beyond the chest.

7

Treatments: Surgery and Chemotherapy

A diagnosis of lung cancer is not a death sentence. In some cases, the patient can be cured (where *cure* is defined as being cancer-free for five years after receiving treatment). But even if the cancer is considered incurable, proper treatment can improve the quality of life by relieving pain and adding months or years to the patient's life. The key to a cure or successful management of lung cancer is getting the best treatment as soon as possible.

The oldest and most effective treatment for cancer is surgery. The goal of surgery is to achieve a complete cure by removing all of the cancer from the body. Surgery is not always possible, however. The tumor may be in a position in the lung that would make the operation too dangerous, or it may already have spread to other parts of the body, or the person may have other heart or lung conditions and may not be strong enough to tolerate surgery.

Other treatments for lung cancer include **chemotherapy** and **radiation therapy**. Radiation therapy aims to control the cancer in the chest by bombarding the tumor with x-rays or other forms of radiation. Chemotherapy seeks to destroy any cancer cells that have spread elsewhere in the body through the administration of drugs that kill cancer cells or stop them from dividing. Sometimes a combination of treatments (called multimodality therapy) is the best approach, especially for patients with early stage disease.

SURGERY

To remove the tumor through surgery offers the best chance of a cure for a lung cancer patient. To choose surgery as the form of treatment, the doctors must be certain that the tumor is small and localized so that the entire tumor can be removed. If any cancerous cells are left behind, the tumor will recur.

The exact location and stage of the cancer must be determined before the operation. An x-ray is usually the first step in the lung cancer diagnosis, but an x-ray alone is not enough. Other tests needed for an accurate diagnosis include imaging tests such as CT, MRI, and PET scans to identify suspicious areas and check for metastases, and a needle biopsy or a bronchoscopy to obtain tissue samples and determine whether the cells are cancerous.

Apart from the type and stage of the tumor, the overall health of the patient must also be considered before deciding on surgery. Lung cancer patients, especially those who are or were heavy smokers, may have other heart or lung conditions that would make the operation too risky. This is why before surgery patients should undergo a test to determine their cardiovascular function to see if their heart is strong enough to go through surgery and a pulmonary function test to determine whether the amount of lung remaining after the operation will allow their survival. Blood and urine tests are also routinely performed to check for infections.

Once the patient is under general anesthesia and before his or her chest is cut open, the surgeon will use either a mediastinoscopy or a thoracoscopy (depending on the location of the tumor) to examine the inside of the chest and take samples to make sure the cancer hasn't moved beyond the lung. If it has, surgery is rarely appropriate.

If the operation is to proceed, the surgeon will use either a side incision (cut) or a front incision to enter the lungs. The side incision runs under the arm, back to front. It is done when the cancer is in the middle or lower portion of the lung. The front incision is done when the tumor is in the upper part of the lungs or if there are tumors in both lungs. To do a front incision, the surgeon may make a vertical split in the sternum (breastbone), or make a cut across the chest. Sometimes it is necessary to remove part or all of one or more ribs to gain access to the tumor.

After making the incision, the surgeon will take samples from the tumor, nearby lung tissue, and lymph nodes. The samples will be examined by a pathologist immediately to find out the kind of tumor and how far it extends into normal tissues and glands and the results reported to the surgeon. Once the surgeon knows which parts are truly cancerous, he or she will **resect** (surgically remove) the tumor along with some surrounding healthy tissue (the **tissue margin**). This margin is important because some cancerous cells may have extended beyond the visible tumor. Most thoracic surgeons also remove all the lymph nodes in the mediastinum even if they seem normal to the touch. Studies have shown that removing all the nodes improves the chance of removing all the cancer, and, therefore, increases the possibility of a cure.

Unlike breast cancer surgery, where usually only the tumor is removed, in lung cancer the whole lobe where the tumor is found is usually removed. To remove a lobe is called a lobectomy. Sometimes, it is necessary to remove two lobes (bilobectomy), or even an entire lung (pneumonectomy).

On rare occasions, when the tumor is in one of the main airways only, it might be possible to remove only a section of an airway and the nearby tissue and join the remaining sections of the airway together. This operation, called sleeve resection, preserves more of the lung that a normal lobectomy does.

On the other side of the spectrum, an extensive resection may be needed if the cancer is more advanced. During an extensive resection, not only the lobes are removed but also the chest wall, ribs, the pleural membrane that surrounds the lungs, the diaphragm, and other affected areas.

The hope with surgery is for the patient to be cured. Unfortunately, there is always the possibility that some cancerous cells will be left behind. To minimize this risk, a pathologist's examination of the visible cancer, the lymph nodes, and the tissue margins removed further determines the kind of tumor and how far it extends into normal tissues and glands. If the pathologist finds any sign of cancer in the lymph nodes, there is a good chance that the cancer has spread beyond the chest, and the patient will be advised to go through chemotherapy. If the cancer is found in the tissue margins, many surgeons suggest radiation.

Even if no cancer is detected in these samples, it is very important to have appropriate follow-up monitoring because anyone who has had lung cancer once is at risk for a recurrence. Regular check-ups, including CT scans, are highly recommended.

INTO THE FUTURE: SURGERY

The detection of smaller lung tumors, due to the high sensitivity of the CT scans, may allow the use of less invasive surgical procedures in the near future. Among the new surgical techniques under investigation are video-assisted thoracic surgery (VATS) and photodynamic therapy (PDT).

In VATS the viewing and surgical instruments are inserted through small incisions between the ribs without the need for opening the chest. Several days before the PDT procedure the patient is injected with a drug that makes cells more sensitive to light. The drug affects both normal and cancerous cells, but stays longer in cancerous cells. During the operation, a laser tool is inserted into the airway via a bronchoscope. The laser targets the sensitized cells of the tumor and kills them. After the operation, the patient should avoid the sun completely for a month, because the cells continue to be abnormally sensitive to light and the patient can be seriously burnt if exposed.

Figure 7.1 In photodynamic therapy, the patient is given a photosensitive drug containing cancer-killing substances, which are absorbed by cancer cells. They are then activated by a light beam. © John Crawford/National Cancer Institute

Figure 7.2 Chemotherapy drugs. © Bill Branson/National Cancer Institute

CHEMOTHERAPY

The ancient Greeks were the first to treat cancer with drugs. Yet chemotherapy as we understand it today did not begin until the 1940s with the use of nitrogen mustard to fight cancer cells.[71] Since then, more effective antitumor drugs have been developed to kill cancerous cells or prevent them from dividing.

Every cell, whether normal or cancerous, goes through a continuous process of change: It grows and then divides into two daughter cells. In turn, these two cells grow, rest, and then divide again. The drugs used in chemotherapy are designed to interrupt this cycle and stop the cells from dividing. Since cancer cells divide more frequently than normal cells, they're more vulnerable to chemotherapy drugs.

Chemotherapy drugs work through different mechanisms, attacking the cells at different stages of their life cycle:[72]

- Antimetabolite drugs imitate normal cell nutrients. The cell takes the drug instead of the normal nutrient, and starves to death when it cannot use it.

- Alkylating agents cause mutations in the cell's DNA and prevent DNA replication. Mustard gas, the first drug used to treat tumors in the 1940s, is an alkylating agent.

- Antitumor antibiotics insert themselves into the strands of DNA and either break the DNA molecule or inhibit the DNA-directed synthesis of RNA. Either way, the cell is disabled.

- Alkaloids prevent the formation of chromosome spindles necessary for cell division.

- Hormonal agents inhibit the growth of some cancers by binding to proteins inside the cancer cells. By doing this, they signal the cells to die.

- Biologic response modifiers disrupt processes that are key to the growth or spread of cancer cells.

To target as many cancer cells as possible, a combination of drugs is usually given. For instance, drugs that attack cells independently of their stage in their life cycle may be given first to reduce the size of the tumor. This may activate the rest of the cells to divide. When they do, other drugs that attack dividing cells will be given.

The drugs used in chemotherapy are very powerful. The line between a therapeutic and a toxic dose is so fine and the consequences of the wrong dose so severe that the doses, schedules, and reaction of the patient to the drugs must be carefully monitored.

Due to this toxicity, chemotherapy is usually given in cycles, with rest periods in between to allow normal cells time to recover and to minimize side effects.

Ways to Administer Chemotherapy

Although some newer chemotherapy drugs can be taken orally in pill or liquid form, most chemotherapy for lung cancer is administered intravenously—through a needle in a vein. One way to administer the drug into the vein is to insert a needle directly into a vein in the hand or forearm every time. But this is not very practical. Some people have small veins, and even with those who don't, it may be difficult to find new veins after several sessions. Also, some drugs could burn the skin, while others are more effective when delivered to larger blood vessels.

This is why the better delivery of the drugs is to have a catheter, a plastic tube (Figure 7.3), implanted under the skin in the chest or in an arm or leg. The drug can be delivered through the catheter either by injection or by slow drip (continuous infusion) over hours or even days. Other fluids, such as nutritional formulas, antibiotics, blood or platelet transfusions, antinausea drugs, or painkilling narcotics can also be delivered through the catheter.

Sometimes, the catheter is attached to a metal or plastic disk—called a port—that is then placed under the skin (Figure 7.3). The port is filled by placing a special needle through the skin into the disk. Again, chemotherapy drugs, antibiotics, or nutrients can also be delivered through the port into a large vein.

Chemotherapy Side Effects

Chemotherapy affects cancer cells because cancer cells divide more rapidly than most normal cells. But the drugs are not selective: Normal cells that grow and divide rapidly will also be affected. That is why the bone marrow (where blood cells are made), the cells in the lining of the digestive system (mouth, stomach, and bowels), the reproductive system, and the hair follicles are particularly affected by chemotherapy. Most normal cells recover after the therapy ends, and the side effects caused by the drugs eventually go away. Unfortunately, some side effects can become chronic.

Port
A metal or plastic disk is implanted under your skin. Attached to the inside is a thin, flexible tube that is threaded into a large vein in your chest. The disk and tube together is called a port.

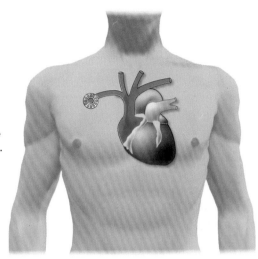

Catheter
A catheter is similar to the tube part of a port. One end is inserted into a vein, but the other end hangs outside your body instead of connecting with a disk just under your skin.

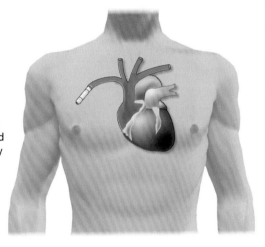

© Infobase Publishing

Figure 7.3 Port and catheter use.

The most frequent side effects of chemotherapy include hair loss, nausea and vomiting, loss of appetite, constipation or diarrhea, and reduced bone marrow activity (myelosuppression) that results in fewer white blood cells, red blood cells, and platelets. Myelosupression causes fatigue, mental confusion, and makes the patient vulnerable to infections.

When chemotherapy affects nerve cells in the brain, it can cause mental confusion, ringing in the ears, hearing impairment, or increased sensitivity to noise; if it affects the nerves of arms and legs, it can cause tingling or a loss of sensation in the fingers and toes.

Other side effects include changes in cardiac or liver function, changes in taste and smell, increased sun sensitivity for the skin, flushing or rashes, and sexual changes, including loss of libido, erectile dysfunction in men, and increased vaginal dryness in women.

Chemotherapy offers a good alternative for treatment in many cases and should not be rejected for fear of the side effects. Most side effects are only temporary and can be relieved with appropriate care and medication. New drugs are under investigation that may offer more effective and safer alternatives in the near future.

8

Treatments: Radiation Therapy, Multimodality Therapy, and Clinical Trials

RADIATION THERAPY

Radiation therapy treats cancer with invisible rays such as x-rays, gamma rays, and electrons. Unlike the ultraviolet rays in sunlight that are blocked by the skin, these rays can penetrate deep inside the body. When they are beamed into the body at low intensity, they create images that can be used for diagnosis. At the higher intensity used in radiation therapy, they can damage or destroy cells by altering their DNA.

Both normal and cancerous cells are affected by radiation. When normal cells are radiated, however, they stop their cell cycle until they have repaired the damage to their DNA (Figure 8.1). Tumor cells, on the other hand, are unable to stop the cell cycle and so they continue to multiply. The resulting cells will have defective chromosomes and most of them will die after a few days.

Roughly 60 percent of lung cancer patients undergo radiation therapy.[73] Traditional candidates for radiation are those patients whose disease is at an advanced stage or who are not strong enough to undergo surgery. In the advanced stages of lung cancer, radiation may improve the patient's quality of life. For instance, radiation may be used to shrink inoperable tumors and ease symptoms such as pain or breathlessness. Because lung tumors are detected at much earlier stages thanks to the sensitivity of CT scans, however, radiation may become increasingly important in the treatment of very small tumors.

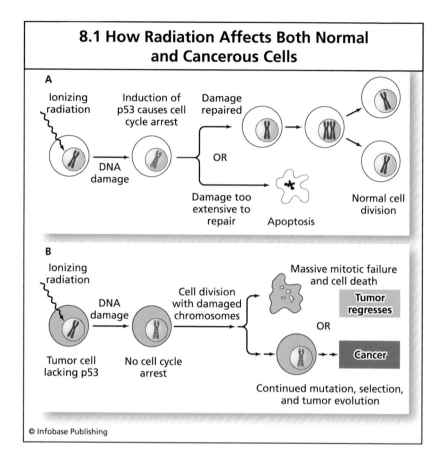

8.1 How Radiation Affects Both Normal and Cancerous Cells

A

Ionizing radiation → DNA damage → Induction of p53 causes cell cycle arrest → Damage repaired → OR → Normal cell division

Damage too extensive to repair → Apoptosis

B

Ionizing radiation → DNA damage → No cell cycle arrest → Cell division with damaged chromosomes → Massive mitotic failure and cell death → **Tumor regresses** OR → **Cancer**

Tumor cell lacking p53

Continued mutation, selection, and tumor evolution

© Infobase Publishing

Radiation is the treatment of choice when the cancer has metastasized to the brain. This is because surgery will be more invasive, and the drugs used in chemotherapy will not pass the **blood-brain barrier** or go into the bones. Surgery, then, would be dangerous and more painful, and chemotherapy will not be effective because bone cells divide very slowly.

Sometimes radiation to the brain is used as a preventive measure before the cancer has actually spread. This procedure, called prophylactic cranial irradiation (PCI), is still controversial due to possible side effects. Recent studies have shown that

PCI increases the odds of survival for SCLC patients whose lung cancer has been successfully treated in the chest.

Radiation is also used

- In combination with surgery: before surgery (neoadjuvant therapy) to shrink the tumor or after surgery (**adjuvant therapy**) to kill any cancer cells that may have remained.

- In combination with chemotherapy: to sensitize tumors so they are more vulnerable to chemotherapy or as consolidation therapy after chemotherapy to kill or disable any remaining cancer cells.

Sources of Radiation: External and Internal

Radiation therapy is usually delivered from an external source. That is, the rays are generated outside the body and aimed at the tumor through an area of the skin, called the radiation port or radiation portal. The source of the external radiation can be a linear accelerator, a machine powered by electricity, or a natural source such as cobalt-60, which is a radioactive form of cobalt that emits gamma rays.

The higher the dose of radiation and the wider the area treated, the larger the chances of killing all the cancer cells. However, increasing the dose and the area treated will also increase the number of normal cells in the path of the rays that are damaged. To diminish the harm done to normal cells and to give the normal cells a chance to recover, the total dose of radiation is usually divided into fractions and administered daily over a period of four to eight weeks.

A new technique, called three-dimensional conformal radiation therapy, provides a better way to decrease the amount of radiation delivered to normal cells during treatment. The radiation beams are aimed at the tumor from multiple angles so that the tumor receives a larger dose than the surrounding tissues. To be able to use this technique, the doctor would have to use advanced x-ray technology and computer image construction to map the exact location, shape, and dimensions of the lung tumor.

Radiation therapy may also be delivered internally. Through a procedure called brachytherapy, the doctor places a small amount of radioactive material inside the body near the tumor or in the area from which the tumor has been removed. At the moment, brachytherapy has a high rate of complications, which makes it less attractive than external

INTO THE FUTURE: RADIATION

Some of the most promising radiation techniques under investigation include radiosurgery, radiation sensitizer and radiation protector drugs, and radioimmunotherapy.

Radiosurgery. Radiosurgery has not been used widely for lung tumors, because the lung moves with every breath and the beam would damage healthy tissue as well. A possible solution, now under investigation, is to implant a radioactive seed in the periphery of the tumor. As the lung expands and contracts during breathing, the seed will move, too, and its movement would be tracked by a computer that would adjust the beam instantly.

Radiation sensitizer and radiation protector drugs. Some drugs could make cancer cells more sensitive to radiation (radiation sensitizers), enhancing its efficacy. Radiation protectors could shield healthy cells from damage, allowing the use of higher doses of radiation against the tumors.

Radioimmunotherapy. The idea behind this technique is to produce antibodies in the laboratory against cancer cells with a radioactive substance attached. Once injected into the body, these radioactive antibodies will selectively bind to and destroy the tumor cells.

radiation in most cases. Still, it may be a valuable tool in relieving severe breathlessness or coughing in the late stages of lung cancer.

Radiation Side Effects

Most side effects of radiation therapy are limited to the area that receives the radiation. Thus, radiation passing through the collarbone, pelvis, breastbone, and skull—the major bone marrow producers—can cause myelosuppression (reduced production of white blood cells, red blood cells, or platelets).

Radiation to the lungs can cause the inflammation of healthy lung tissue. Usually this happens one to two months after the treatment ends. The symptoms of this condition—called radiation pneumonitis—are similar to those of the flu: shortness of breath, coughing, and fever. Steroids, and antibiotics if there is an infection, will relieve these symptoms.

Occasionally radiation treatment causes scars in the lung tissue (radiation fibrosis). The symptoms of radiation fibrosis are similar to those of pneumonitis, but they appear about a year after treatment. Unfortunately, radiation fibrosis is not reversible.

Radiation delivered to the brain can cause confusion, headache, and nausea. These symptoms, if they appear early in the treatment, are usually caused by the swelling of the brain in response to the treatment. Later symptoms, like impaired memory, diminished intellect, inability to concentrate, and personality changes, may be the result of radiation necrosis, or the accumulation of dead tissue from the treated tumor. Both sets of symptoms may be treated with steroids or other drugs.

Radiation can also produce temporary or permanent hair loss in the treated area, or skin irritation. The skin irritation can be more severe after chemotherapy, because some drugs used in chemotherapy may sensitize the skin to radiation (radiation recall).

Other common side effects of radiation include fatigue, soreness when swallowing, and, ironically, an increased risk of cancer at the treated site.

MULTIMODALITY THERAPY

Often the best way to treat lung cancer is through a combination of treatments. The choice of treatments and the order in which to apply them depend on the stage and type of lung cancer.

Treatment of Small Cell Lung Cancer

In most cases, by the time SCLC is diagnosed several tumors are already present throughout both lungs, so surgery is not an option. Instead, a combination of radiation and chemotherapy is used. If SCLC is in the limited stage, the goal of the treatment is to cure the cancer. If the disease has spread, treatment is used to slow its progress and to relieve symptoms.

If SCLC is still at the limited stage—confined to one lung and the mediastinum—a combination of chemotherapy and radiation therapy is recommended. Radiation may be used first to make tumor cells more vulnerable to the chemotherapy, or after chemotherapy to kill or disable any remaining cancer cells.

When SCLC is in the extensive stage (when it has moved beyond the chest), chemotherapy is the preferred initial treatment. Then radiation may be used to treat the metastasis, especially in the brain, bones, or spine. Radiation can also be used to relieve symptoms such as pain or breathlessness, by reducing the tumor that is causing them.

Treatment of Non-Small Cell Lung Cancer (NSCLC)

Surgery is the treatment of choice for stages I and II NSCLC because it offers the best chance for a cure. If the patient cannot withstand surgery or the tumor cannot be removed without affecting a vital organ, however, radiation may be used.

Sometimes, radiation is given before the operation to shrink the tumor (neoadjuvant therapy). It is not usually recommended after surgery, since studies have shown that radiation does not improve survival for people with stage I and II NSCLC.

When the cancer has spread within the chest but is still on the same side as the affected lung (stage IIIA), treatment may begin with surgery, followed by chemotherapy or radiation, or both to kill the remaining cancer cells. As in stages I and II, chemotherapy may be used first to shrink the tumor before surgery or radiation.

When both sides of the chest are involved but the cancer has not metastasized (stage IIIB), a combination of chemotherapy and radiation offers the best hope for long-term survival. Sometimes surgery is possible after this first treatment, followed by chemotherapy to kill any remaining cancer cells.

Once the cancer has spread beyond the chest, the disease is usually not curable, unless both the lung tumor and the metastasis are still small and localized. More often, the goal of the treatment for stage IV NSCLC is to control the spread of the disease and to improve the patient's quality of life. Radiation or chemotherapy is used to shrink tumors that may cause pain, breathlessness, or other symptoms. Radiation is usually used when the metastasis is in the brain or bone.

With the right treatment, patients with stage IV disease can live for five years and longer, and, except for enduring some unpleasant effects during the periods when they are receiving radiation or chemotherapy, they can lead fulfilling lives.

CLINICAL TRIALS

If the standard treatment options available aren't likely to be effective, the doctor might suggest that the patient participate in a **clinical trial**. A clinical trial is a research study conducted to determine whether a new treatment (new drug or new method) is both effective and reasonably safe for people. The treatment plan offered in a clinical trial might involve a new anticancer drug or a combination of treatment methods. Clinical trials are also conducted to study methods for cancer prevention.

Only those drugs and medical devices that pass the clinical trials are considered for approval by the Food and Drug Administration (FDA). Approval by the FDA is necessary before the new treatment can be used as a routine therapy.

Patients who take part in clinical trials are not guinea pigs. New treatments are offered in clinical trials only after extensive laboratory research has demonstrated that they are at least as good as, and potentially much better than, standard therapies. Data from the Center for the Study of Drug Development at Tufts University indicate that out of thousands of compounds that are screened for drug development, only 250 enter preclinical testing, and five of those enter clinical testing.[74]

Clinical trials allow new treatments to develop. Just about every chemotherapy drug and radiation treatment used today as standard therapy was first given as a clinical Phase I trial. Clinical trials are conducted in three phases.

Phase I

The purpose of a Phase I clinical trial is to determine the safest dose for a drug or best method to use when giving a new treatment and to identify side effects. Phase I trials usually enroll a small number of patients, as few as a dozen.

Because the drug or treatment has never been used in humans before, there is no assurance that the tumor will respond. In fact, fewer than five percent of drugs ever get to the next trial phase. This is why participation is restricted to patients with late-stage disease who have no other treatment options, in the hope that the new agent or method might prove effective. Phase I trials may not require the participants to have a particular kind of cancer.

Once the drug shows clear signs of being effective without causing undue risk, it moves on to Phase II.

Phase II

A Phase II trial tries to determine if the treatment is effective in decreasing the size of a tumor. To participate, a patient usually has to have readily measured symptoms or tumors. A Phase II trial also notes the number of patients responding favorably. One or more groups of about 30 to 40 patients are enrolled.

As in Phase I trials, participation is usually limited to patients with advanced disease who don't have other treatment options. Phase II trials may be specific for lung cancer, but usually not for a particular type of cancer.

Phase III

Only those treatments shown to have strong positive effects and acceptable side effects in Phases I and II are tested in a Phase III trial.

A Phase III trial compares the new treatment to existing treatments. Usually these trials are specific to lung cancer and sometimes even to a type of lung cancer. Hundreds of patients are enrolled in this phase and assigned at random to receive the standard treatment, the therapy under investigation, or a placebo (no treatment at all).

The clinical trial ends when the number of patients needed to validate the experiment has completed the treatment. It may end sooner, though, if investigators learn in the middle of the trial that either the new treatment or the old one is clearly superior.

After a new treatment has finished a Phase III trial and received FDA approval, further trials can be done to learn more about its possible side and long-term effects, to find out the best way to administer the treatment, or to see how it compares to other approved treatments.

9

Biological Therapies

PROMISING NEW THERAPIES

All of the cancer treatments we have seen so far try to rid the body of cancer by cutting the cancer out, poisoning it with drugs, or killing it with radiation. Just like getting rid of weeds from a garden, it is hard to eliminate every single one of them or not to kill some good plants in the process. Surgery can rarely eliminate every metastasis, and the drugs used in chemotherapy and the radiation rays that kill cancer cells are generally toxic to normal cells as well. And, as with weeds, even if only a few cancerous cells remain, they can proliferate again and reproduce the disease.

To effectively cure cancer, more powerful and selective ways of directly killing all cancer cells are needed. With this goal in mind, researchers are designing therapies to take advantage of the knowledge of the molecular bases of cancer gained during the last few decades to target some property of the cancer cells that distinguishes them from normal cells.

One of these new strategies, **immunotherapy**, tries to get the body itself to fight the cancer by activating the immune system. Another approach focuses on the cancer cells' need for a blood supply to grow (**anti-angiogenesis therapy).** Other therapies try to fix the mutations in the cell's DNA responsible for the transformation of the normal cell into a cancer cell (**gene therapy**); to stop the mutated gene from being made into a protein (**antisense RNA therapy**); or to restore the telomerase activity in the transformed cells, because the lack of telomerase activity is believed to be the reason cancer cells do not stop dividing or are "immortal."

Immunotherapy

When something foreign, such as bacteria or viruses, enters the body, several kinds of white blood cells (leukocytes) go into action to fight the invaders. The leukocytes involved in this defense mechanism, called the immune response, include the phagocytes (neutrophils, monocytes, eosinophils), the lymphocytes (**T-cells** and **B-cells**), and the basophils (Figure 9.1).

The neutrophils are the first cells to arrive at the site of the infection. They do not survive for long, but they may overcome the invaders by their sheer number: Billions of neutrophils are produced each day.

The monocytes arrive next. Upon encountering the invader, they grow and swell until they become huge macrophages that are able to engulf the foreign particles. After they have digested these foreign particles, they carry pieces of them (**antigens**) on their membranes. As the monocytes move about the body with the antigens on their membrane, they eventually encounter T-cells that recognize these antigens and lock into them like a key in a lock. When this happens, the T-cell releases interleukin II (interleukin is one of the immune system hormones). Interleukin II stimulates the rapid cell divisions of the T- and B-cells that specifically match this antigen. The role of the T-cells (cytotoxic T-cells, or killer T-cells) is to look for cells that carry that specific antigen and destroy them (Figure 9.1). The B-cells bind to any invaders bearing matching antigens but they need the help of T-cells to destroy them. B-cells attack not only cells but also bacteria, fungi, and viruses.

Once they are stimulated by the T-cells, B-cells divide and produce plasma cells and memory cells. The plasma cells live only a few days, but while they are alive, they constantly produce antibodies—proteins that specifically recognize and bind

9.1 The Immune Response

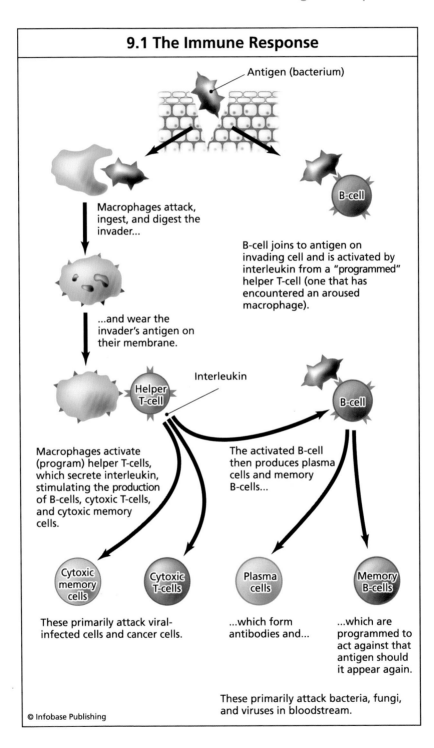

Antigen (bacterium)

B-cell

Macrophages attack, ingest, and digest the invader...

B-cell joins to antigen on invading cell and is activated by interleukin from a "programmed" helper T-cell (one that has encountered an aroused macrophage).

...and wear the invader's antigen on their membrane.

Interleukin

Helper T-cell

B-cell

Macrophages activate (program) helper T-cells, which secrete interleukin, stimulating the production of B-cells, cytoxic T-cells, and cytoxic memory cells.

The activated B-cell then produces plasma cells and memory B-cells...

Cytoxic memory cells

Cytoxic T-cells

Plasma cells

Memory B-cells

These primarily attack viral-infected cells and cancer cells.

...which form antibodies and...

...which are programmed to act against that antigen should it appear again.

These primarily attack bacteria, fungi, and viruses in bloodstream.

to the antigen. The memory cells live for years. If this same antigen invades the body again, the memory B-cell will recognize it and (with help from the helper T-cells) immediately start producing new plasma cells and memory cells. In this way, the later invasion is beaten back before it starts.

As we have seen, the human body is well equipped to recognize and destroy foreign cells, yet it does not attack cancer

HELP IN UNUSUAL PLACES: SHARK CARTILAGE

Years ago, when lung cancer patients who had run out of traditional treatment options took shark cartilage in the hope of being cured, doctors shook their head in disbelief.

Today Neovostat®, an antiogenesis inhibitor extracted from shark cartilage, is one of the new drugs being tested in the treatment of lung cancer. Squalamine, a similar drug derived from shark liver, is in clinical trials throughout the world.

Cartilage has the potential to inhibit the development of new blood vessels and it also seems to act directly to slow tumor cell growth. Researchers are still looking for the precise factors responsible for these effects in the cartilage. And since cartilage constitutes a small amount (approximately only six percent) of body weight in sharks, it is no surprise that experiments are being conducted with these animals.

Phase I and II clinical trials of Neovostat have established the drug's excellent safety and tolerability. Some lung and breast cancer patients have been taking Neovostat for almost four years now without any serious side effects. The only thing they complain about is its fishy smell.

Source: Lane, William I., and Linda Comac. *Sharks Don't Get Cancer.* Garden City Park, N.Y.: Avery Publishing Group, Inc., 1992. Dooley, Joseph F., and Marian Betancourt. *The Coming Cancer Breakthroughs: What You Need to Know About the Latest Cancer Treatment Options.* New York: Kensington Books, 2002.

cells. The reason the body does not destroy cancer cells is that cancer cells are not outsiders. They are simply transformed body cells. This fact allows them to grow in the body and evade its defenses for years. The plan behind immunotherapy is to find a way to make the body's immune system recognize and kill cancer cells. The three main approaches to do so are cancer vaccines, monoclonal antibodies, and the use of cytokines (immune system hormones).

Cancer Vaccines

Vaccines against microorganisms are preventive. The body is injected with a dead or weakened microorganism or parts of the microorganism. During this first infection, the body produces memory cells that will prevent the body from becoming sick from a future infection by the same microorganism.

Cancer vaccines, on the other hand, are used after the person has cancer. The intention of a cancer vaccine is to stimulate the T-cells against the cancer cells that are already in the body.

Some tumor cell vaccines use cancer cells from the patient (autologous vaccine). Others use cells from other patients (allogeneic vaccine). The cancer cells are killed and then injected back into the patient. The dead cells cannot form tumors, but the antigens on their surface can stimulate an immune response. Other vaccines (antigen vaccines) use only individual antigens, rather than the whole tumor cell. Because the genetic code of many antigens is known, the antigens can be produced in the lab. Some antigens cause an immune response against one kind of cancer, while others cause reactions against several kinds. Sometimes several antigens are combined in a single vaccine.

When antigens are first injected into the body, they produce the desired immune response. But over time, they become less effective because antibodies rapidly bind and destroy them. DNA vaccines can solve this problem by having bits of DNA injected into certain cells in the body. These altered cells will produce the antigen all the time, keeping the immune system active against the cancer cells that have this antigen.

Monoclonal Antibodies (MABs)

Antibodies are proteins produced by the B-cell lymphocytes against a specific part of a foreign structure (the antigen). The antibodies have two parts: a variable part that recognizes the antigen and a constant part that is recognized by other cells of the immune system, such as monocytes, macrophages, and neutrophils. Once these cells recognize the antibody, they attack and destroy the structure to which the antibody is attached.

Monoclonal antibodies (MABs) are antibodies designed **in vitro** (in a laboratory rather than the human body) against a specific protein of the cancer cell. MABs are created by injecting human cancer cells into mice. The B-cell lymphocytes from mice that produce antigens against human cancer cells are purified and cloned. Each clone will produce only one highly specific antibody (hence, the term *monoclonal antibody*). When injected into a cancer patient, the MABs bind to tumor-associated proteins on the cancer cell surface. MABs can be used for cancer diagnosis (the MABs will detect cancer cells in blood or tissue taken from the patient) or to target the tumor for destruction in vivo (in the body). MABs can be used alone (unconjugated antibodies), linked to a potent cell-killing drug (antibody-targeted chemotherapy), or linked to radioisotopes (radioisotope-conjugated MABs). There are more than 70 MABs now in clinical trials, half of them for cancer, according to the Pharmaceutical Research and Manufacturers of America.[75] To treat cancer, the aim is to kill cells. But the MABs used to date seem not to kill but merely to slow down the cancer cells. In most cases, they don't seem to be any more effective than chemotherapy in bringing about **remission**, though they do have fewer side effects.

Cytokines

Cytokines are immune system hormones—substances that the cells in the body use to communicate with each other. Cytokines are being studied as a therapeutic means of altering the interaction between the body's immune system and the cancer, thus improving the body's ability to fight the disease.

Some cytokines occur naturally in the body. Others that imitate or influence the natural ones can be made in the laboratory.

There are several types of cytokines under investigation for cancer therapy. Among them:

Interferons may stimulate B-cells and T-cells, thus strengthening the fighting function of the immune system, or act directly on the cancer cells, either by inhibiting their growth or promoting their development into cells with more normal behavior. Interleukins stimulate the growth and functions of many immune cells that can destroy cancer cells.

Tumor necrosis factor also stimulates the immune system increasing its ability to fight cancer.

Colony-stimulating factors stimulate the bone marrow cells to divide and develop into white blood cells, platelets, and red blood cells. They can be used to counteract the damaging effects on white blood cells caused by the cancer drugs used in chemotherapy.

Anti-angiogenesis Therapy

All the cells in the body, including the cancer cells, need oxygen to live, and a blood supply that will provide them with oxygen. That is why a tumor needs new blood vessels if it is to grow to more than a millimeter in size. Without new blood vessels the tumor will die.

Several approaches are currently under investigation to stop the growth of new blood vessels in tumors.

One of the approaches uses angiogenesis inhibitors that block the local signals (called angiogenic growth factors) necessary for the growth of new vessels.

Another kind of agent under investigation targets certain cell-surface markers that are only present in those cells that are in the process of forming new vessels. Existing blood vessels would not be affected by these agents.

Therapies that block angiogenesis have the advantage of not being specific to one type of cancer cell. They should block tumor growth in many different types of cancer. There are at least 11 compounds now in clinical trials that may target angiogenesis.[76]

Gene Therapy

Gene therapy involves the insertion of a gene into a cell. Since cancer is caused by mutations that make certain genes either overactive or underactive, gene therapy could possibly fix the problem by replacing the faulty gene or genes with a correct version.

Laboratory studies of the p53 gene indicate that the technique does work. The normal p53 gene puts the brakes on cell growth and forces cells to commit suicide if their DNA is damaged. A mutation of the p53 gene is one of the causes in the transformation of normal cells into cancer cells in lung, ovarian, head and neck, and colorectal cancers, among others. Introducing a normal p53 gene into a cancer cell with a mutated p53 gene has been shown to restore the p53 gene function, causing cell death or a cessation of its growth.

Gene therapy strategy is to deliver genes to cancer cells that will directly or indirectly kill them. One approach is to introduce genes that will synthesize enzymes that activate chemotherapy drugs. Another approach under investigation is to insert certain immune system genes into cancer cells to better stimulate an immune response against the cancer.

Although the idea of gene therapy is simple, delivering the genes is problematic. Delivery vehicles, called vectors, direct genes into the proper cells and get them to function once they are there. The most common vectors are deactivated viruses, such as adenovirus, and synthetic particles called liposomes.

These vectors are not perfect. It is not yet possible to get the desired genes into all of the cancer cells in a patient's body. Until now, clinical studies of gene therapy have focused on treatment of particular sites in the body, such as those confined areas where genes can be delivered more efficiently.

Antisense RNA Therapy

Most diseases are caused by incorrect or excess production of proteins. Information to produce these proteins is contained in genes in the DNA. In order to make a protein, the cell first makes an RNA copy of the gene containing the information for that protein. This copy is called messenger RNA (mRNA). The mRNA is then read by the cell and translated into a protein. An antisense drug is a piece of RNA that complements the mRNA, binding specifically to it and preventing the mRNA from being translated into the protein. Because of its specificity, antisense RNA therapy should be less toxic than the traditional drugs used in chemotherapy.

Inhibition of Telomerase Activity

All DNA strands in human chromosomes are capped by telomeres, which are extra bits of DNA that snap off piece by piece every time a cell divides. Once the telomeres are gone, the cell stops dividing and dies. So, in a sense, a telomere is like a clock that regulates how many times an individual cell can divide.

In cancer cells, the telomeres are replenished by an enzyme called telomerase. Because the telomeres do not disappear, the cells divide indefinitely. Telomerase activity has been detected in almost all human tumors.

Researchers are studying ways to inhibit telomerase activity to force the cancer cells to age and die like normal cells. They believe this may be a way to stop the growth of many types of cancer.

Perhaps in the future scientists will be able to compare the DNA of the cancer cells of a patient with the DNA of his or her normal cells and identify the mutations that produced the transformation. Once this is done, doctors will be able to select the exact medication that will alter the patient's cancer gene profile, and either change the cell back to normal by turning some particular gene off or destroy the cancer cells by turning on a particular gene. In this way, the treatment of cancer will be free of all the unpleasant side effects of current anticancer drugs.[77]

However, until this scenario becomes a reality, prevention (by avoiding environmental factors, especially tobacco smoke) and screening (to detect cancer in the earlier, more treatable stages) are the best alternatives.

10

Further Treatments and End-of-Life Care

COMPLEMENTARY AND ALTERNATIVE MEDICINE (CAM)

After being diagnosed with lung cancer, many patients turn to **alternative therapies**, such as herbs and vitamins, exercise, massage, or folk remedies. According to a survey published in 2000 in the *Journal of Clinical Oncology*,[78] most people do so to expand their options and because these therapies make them feel hopeful.

The National Cancer Institute has grouped all those approaches that are not a part of the conventional medical treatment in the United States under the name of **Complementary and Alternative Medicine (CAM)** treatments. In this context, a technique may be considered a **complementary therapy** when used *in addition to* conventional treatment, and a technique may be considered as an alternative therapy when used *instead of* conventional treatment.

Most physicians, who until recently scorned any alternative treatment, are becoming more open to them. For instance, most doctors today accept that some of these treatments—such as relaxation (stress reduction exercises), support groups, or massages—can improve the well-being and quality of life of cancer patients. Yet they remain wary of other treatments, and not without reason. Such treatments have not been submitted to the clinical trial system, and neither alternative practitioners nor dietary supplements and herbal remedies are subjected to the traditional safeguards that protect consumers. Unlike medical physicians, alternative practitioners do not have to be licensed and, unlike drugs, dietary supplements or herbal remedies are not reviewed by the Food and Drug Administration (FDA).

Physicians also fear that patients will abandon conventional treatments that could prolong their lives, reduce symptoms, or even cure their disease in favor of an unproven CAM therapy. In some cases, an alternative treatment can interfere in known or unknown ways with conventional treatment.

PSYCHOLOGICAL APPROACHES

It is a fact that the mind affects the body. Watching a scary movie can make the heart beat faster, and it has been documented in scientific studies that taking a placebo (a pill or treatment that, unknown to the patient, has no medical value) makes some patients feel better.

Some techniques that help channel the power of the mind to help the body have been proven safe and effective and are generally accepted today by the conventional practitioners. These techniques can help the body relax and improve the person's mood; they may also help relieve pain and nausea. In general, they can improve the patient's quality of life and, as a consequence, his or her health. Support groups, relaxation, meditation, hypnosis, and imagery are among the complementary techniques that use the mind-body connection as a tool in the treatment of cancer.

Support Groups

A study conducted in the 1970s by Stanford University psychiatrist David Spiegel with breast cancer patients showed that women with breast cancer who joined a support group were less anxious, less depressed, and less exhausted than women not attending a support group. The average survival time proved to be nearly twice as long for those in support groups, and the only three women alive ten years after the study had all been in support groups.

This is not so surprising if we consider that support and encouragement improve our mood. When patients are happier, they are likely to sleep and eat better, which will make them healthier. If they are healthier, they will be able to tolerate cancer treatment better and will be less likely to stop the treatment.

Meditation

Meditation is the act of focusing the thoughts in the mind. Research has shown that meditation, a mental and physical relaxation technique, lowers blood pressure, reduces stress, and counters chronic pain and insomnia. Meditation can help decrease some of the side effects (nausea and vomiting) related to chemotherapy, alleviate pain, and decrease the anxiety in cancer patients.

Techniques used for relaxation include progressive muscle relaxation, which involves concentrating successively on every part of the body to let go of tension and tightness; biofeedback; and dance, music, and art therapy.

Hypnosis, Self-Hypnosis, and Imagery

Hypnosis and self-hypnosis do not imply a loss of consciousness, but rather involve deep relaxation. Once under hypnosis, the patient can focus his or her attention on a particular goal such as clearing away the pain or reducing nausea.

The imagination can be used to visualize helpful or distracting imagery. These images can help the person relax during a medical procedure, or help him or her connect with an inner voice to visualize a desired outcome, such as the cancer cells being destroyed. Studies suggest that imagery can help manage pain, nausea, anxiety, and stress.

SPIRITUAL APPROACHES

Spiritual approaches to treating cancer include prayer, contemplation, laying on of hands, and any other forms of spiritual imagery or inner dialogue. Spirituality goes beyond being a member of a particular religion; it implies having a deep relationship with the self. Achieving deeper levels of awareness may

DANGERS OF ALTERNATIVE THERAPIES

In a survey of 453 patients being treated for cancer at the M.D. Anderson Cancer Center in Texas, 83 percent reported using at least one complementary or alternative therapy. Of those using CAM, 65 percent did not tell their oncologists. Such a lack of communication can put these patients at risk for dangerous, even deadly, interactions between their conventional treatment and the alternative ones.

Vitamins A, C, and E are beneficial in healthy individuals because they protect the body against oxidation, a process that can damage DNA. But the goal of chemotherapy and radiation therapy is to damage the DNA in the cancerous cells. Taking vitamins can interfere with the effect of these treatments.

Blue-green algae and other herbal products that contain vitamin K promote blood clotting. But many lung cancer patients take medication that inhibits clotting (blood thinners) to prevent the formation of blood clots that could cause a pulmonary embolism, a heart attack, or a stroke.

Extracts from the tree Ginkgo biloba, on the other hand, impair blood clotting. This could be a problem during surgery and other procedures that cause bleeding.

St. John's wort, which is taken to treat depression and anxiety, may intensify the effects of certain anesthetics and painkillers and can cause problems during and after surgery.

A very strict low-fat vegetarian diet can be beneficial for some people, but it could be dangerous for cancer patients who have already lost a lot of weight due to their illness.

Source: Henschke, Claudia I., and Peggy McCarty, with Sarah Wernick. *Lung Cancer: Myths, Facts, Choices—and Hope*. New York: W. W. Norton & Company, 2002, p. 248.

help the person move beyond feelings of helplessness to feelings of empowerment. Cultivating inner peace, tranquility, and joy can bring balance emotionally and physically, which in turn may decrease the stress of living with cancer, and help the healing.

PHYSICAL APPROACHES
Exercise

It has not been proven that exercise helps prevent cancer. However, exercise has been shown to have a positive effect on depression, and this may help the patient through one of the mind-body pathways. Also, cancer treatment seems to work better on patients who are in good physical condition. Exercise, then, will benefit the patient indirectly by improving his/her fitness.

Massage

Massage—stroking, rubbing, or kneading the muscles—can relieve pain, reduce stress and anxiety, and improve mood. Cancer patients should always consult their doctor first, and notify their therapist of their condition. In general, only light versions of massage are recommended for most cancer patients. Pressure in areas of bone metastasis and in sensitive skin areas that may be present after radiation therapy should be avoided. Another concern regarding massage for cancer patients is that the massage may, in theory, stimulate the lymphatic spread of certain cancers.

Yoga

Yoga involves gentle stretching, breathing techniques, and relaxation. It improves both the physical and psychological well-being of the person and leads to a deep inner peace that can help in the healing process. Cancer patients, however, should consult an experienced instructor to learn to avoid those positions that could be uncomfortable because of their disease or treatment.

TRADITIONAL CHINESE MEDICINE

Traditional Chinese medicine includes acupuncture, acupressure, *Qi gong*, and herbal medicine.

According to Chinese philosophy, these methods manipulate the life force, or *qi*, (pronounced "chee")[79], which flows in the body along pathways called meridians. Each meridian is associated with a specific organ or body system. Disease is considered to be the result of an imbalance of energy in the meridians and their associated organs.

Expert practitioners can manipulate the flow of *qi* with acupuncture, where fine, flexible needles are inserted in specific sites along the meridian points or with acupressure, by exerting pressure on specific sites, or by the use of *Qi gong*, a form of movement and meditation.

Herbal medicine is perhaps the main component of traditional Chinese medicine. Although some published reports claim that Chinese herbal medicine is effective in treating certain types of cancer, however, this has not been proven according to Western standards. Herbal medicine should be used with caution: The ingredients in plant extracts could have harmful interactions with other medications, and, because their preparation has not been standardized, not all the pills contain the same amount of an active ingredient.

ADDITIONAL TREATMENTS

There are many other unconventional treatments for lung cancer. Usually, as is the case with those mentioned above, their goal is to relieve symptoms or side effects, or to improve the efficacy of the standard medical treatment. But in some cases a therapy is promoted as being able to cure the disease. Patients should be extremely cautious before agreeing to these treatments and should always consult their doctor first.

FOLLOW-UP CARE

Lung cancer patients, even those who are pronounced "cured" (their tumor has been surgically removed and no cancer has been detected in the tissue margins) or "in complete remission" (no cancer is detected after chemotherapy, radiation, or both for five consecutive years) need follow-up care after their treatment is over.

This is because survivors are at higher risk for a **recurrent cancer** (reemergence of the original cancer) or a new primary cancer (a new, unrelated tumor) because:

- Cancer cells may remain after treatment even when no tumor is detected.

- Some of the molecular changes that caused the tumor may be present in other cells in the lung, and, especially if the cause of the cancer (such as smoke or exposure to carcinogens) is still present, these cells could acquire the extra mutation that will make them cancerous.

- Some cancer treatments (radiation and certain kinds of chemotherapy) may damage cells and increase the risk of subsequent cancers.

According to the American Society of Clinical Oncology, follow-up care may include a CT scan, an MRI test, or a PET scan soon after the treatment is finished. The doctors will compare the results of these tests with the earlier tests to evaluate the patient's present condition. Later follow-up examinations may include chest x-rays, bronchoscopy, and a complete blood cell count.

Some changes in the patient's lifestyle (eating well and exercising more) may also help him or her to stay healthier and feel better. It is also important that he or she review his or her risk factors to minimize exposure to carcinogens, especially cigarette smoke.

Many people continue smoking even after they have been diagnosed with lung cancer. They may think that quitting will make no difference now that they already have the disease. They are wrong.

Smoking increases the likelihood of developing complications during standard lung cancer treatment—surgery, chemotherapy, and radiation therapy. Smoking also worsens chemotherapy or radiation-related nausea and fatigue. Smoking causes the accumulation of mucus in the lungs, which provokes especially painful coughing after surgery, and other complications.

In addition, smoking increases the risk of other diseases, such as heart disease, stroke, and emphysema, and interferes with breathing. Most patients who have lost or had part of their lung tissue damaged during treatment are more susceptible to the further loss of lung function that smoking causes.

Smoking increases the risk of developing a secondary lung cancer in another part of the lung. Many chemicals in tobacco smoke are potent mutagens that could lead some lung cells that are already in the precancerous stages to become cancer cells.

END-OF-LIFE CARE

Sometimes cancer is detected too late and is already too advanced to treat. In some cases treatment doesn't stop the tumor's growth or metastases are found during treatment, and treatment must be discontinued. When the cancer cannot be cured or controlled, patients must learn to live with the knowledge that their time is limited.

Unlike those who die unexpectedly, patients with cancer have some time left to prepare, to say good-bye to family and friends, and to leave a personal legacy such as creating a journal or writing letters or starting a special project in their community.

For the final stage of the illness, many doctors recommend a hospice program to provide end-of-life care. Hospice programs offer a team of doctors, nurses, home health aides, social workers, and religious or other counselors to provide medical and emotional support to the patient as death approaches. Symptoms such as pain, breathlessness, and emotional agitation may be controlled through medication (usually narcotic painkillers and sedatives), but all treatments are given for comfort, not to prolong life. Hospice care can be given at home or at hospitals, nursing homes, or special hospice facilities.

Hospice programs also provide support for caregivers to help them care for the patient. Sometimes friends and relatives feel so overwhelmed by their emotions when someone they love is dying that they avoid talking about the issue or visiting. But there are ways they can offer their support. They might work on a project with the patient, read aloud, talk, give a massage, hold hands, or just sit by the patient's side. If the caregiver is out of ideas, he or she can always ask the patient for guidance. The hospice team can also serve as a resource.

Friends should encourage the patient to share his or her thoughts and feelings and listen to him or her, even when what he or she says is painful. They should remember it is all right to cry or express sadness.

Death is a part of life. Despite the grief and sense of loss that being diagnosed with late-stage lung cancer can bring, many patients are grateful for the time they are given to prepare, to do what really matters to them, and to bring a sense of meaning and closure to their lives.

Notes

1. Centers for Disease Control and Prevention, *Lung Cancer Statistics.* Available online. URL: http://www.cdc. gov/cancer/lung/statistics.htm#statistics. Downloaded on May 10, 2006.
2. American Lung Association, *Trends in Lung Cancer.* Available online. URL: http://www.lungusa.org/atf/cf/{7A8D42 C2-FCCA-4604-8ADE-7F5D5E762256}/lc1.pdf.
3. Ibid.
4. Weinberg, Robert A. *Racing to the Beginning of the Road: The Search for the Origin of Cancer.* New York: W.H. Freeman and Company, 1996, p. 21.
5. MedicineWorld.org. "History of Cancer." Available online. URL: http://medicineworld.org/cancer/ history.html. Downloaded May 8, 2006.
6. Diamond, John W., M.D., and Lee W. Cowden, M.D. with Burton Goldberg. *Burton Goldberg Presents an Alternative Medicine Definitive Guide to Cancer.* Tiburon, Calif.: Future Medicine Publishing, Inc., 1997, pp. 518-519.
7. Coleman, Norman C., M.D. *Understanding Cancer: A Patient's Guide to Diagnosis, Prognosis, and Treatment.* Baltimore: The Johns Hopkins University Press, 1998, p. 27.
8. Ibid., pp. 28–29.
9. Bruce Alberts, et al. "Cancer as a Microevolutionary Process." Available online. URL: http://www.ncbi.nlm.nih. gov/entrez/query.fcgi?cmd=Search&db= books&doptcmdl=GenBookHL&term= microevolutionary+AND+mboc4%5Bb ook%5D+AND+374864%5Buid%5D&r id=mboc4.section.4259. Downloaded on May 8, 2004.
10. Wallace, Robert A. *Biology: The World of Life.* New York: HarperCollins Publishers, 1992, pp. 182-184.
11. Wolfe, Stephen L. *Introduction to Cell and Molecular Biology.* Belmont, Calif.: BrooksCole/Thomson, 1995, pp. 25-26.
12. National Center for Biotechnology Information, National Library of Medicine, National Institutes of Health, "Finding the Cancer-Critical Gene."

Available online. URL: http://www.ncbi. nlm.nih.gov/entrez/query.fcgi?cmd =Search&db=books&doptcmdl= GenBookHL&term=cancer-critical+ genes+AND+mboc4%5Bbook%5D+ AND+374898%5Buid%5D&rid= mboc4.section.4309. Downloaded on May 8, 2006.
13. James D. Watson, and Frank H.C. Crick, 1953. "Molecular Structure of Nucleic Acids. A Structure for Deoxyribose Nucleic Acid," *Nature* 171: 737. Available online. URL: http://www.nature.com/nature/dna50/ watsoncrick.pdf. Downloaded on May 8, 2006.
14. Bruce Alberts, et al. "Cancer as a Microevolutionary Process." Available online. URL: http://www.ncbi.nlm. nih.gov/entrez/query.fcgi?cmd=Search &db=books&doptcmdl=GenBookHL& term=microevolutionary+AND+ mboc4%5Bbook%5D+AND+374864 %5Buid%5D&rid=mboc4.section.4259. Downloaded on May 8, 2006.
15. Bruce Alberts, et al. "Cancer as a Microevolutionary Process." Available online. URL: http://www.ncbi. nlm.nih.gov/entrez/query.fcgi?cmd= Search&db=books&doptcmdl=GenBoo kHL&term=microevolutionary+ AND+mboc4%5Bbook%5D+AND +374864%5Buid%5D&rid=mboc4. section.4259. Downloaded on May 8, 2006.
16. Wolfe, Stephen L. *Introduction to Cell and Molecular Biology.* Belmont, Calif.: BrooksCole/Thomson, 1995, p. 649.
17. Henschke, Claudia I., and Peggy McCarty, with Sarah Wernick. *Lung Cancer: Myths, Facts, Choices—and Hope.* New York: W.W. Norton & Company, 2002, p. 33
18. Wolfe, Stephen L. *Introduction to Cell and Molecular Biology.* Belmont, Calif.: BrooksCole/Thomson 1995, p. 649.
19. Coleman, Norman C., M.D. *Understanding Cancer. A Patient's Guide*

to *Diagnosis, Prognosis, and Treatment.* Baltimore: The Johns Hopkins University Press, 1998, pp. 13-14.

20. Henschke, Claudia I., and Peggy McCarty, with Sarah Wernick. *Lung Cancer: Myths, Facts, Choices—and Hope.* New York: W.W. Norton & Company, 2002, p. 33.

21. Wolfe, Stephen L. *Introduction to Cell and Molecular Biology.* Belmont, Calif.: BrooksCole/Thomson 1995, p. 648.

22. Ibid., p. 632.

23. Ibid., p. 674.

24. Henschke, Claudia I. and Peggy McCarty, with Sarah Wernick. *Lung Cancer: Myths, Facts, Choices—and Hope.* New York: W.W. Norton & Company, 2002, p. 32.

25. American Lung Association. "Smoking 101 Fact Sheet." Available online. URL: http://www.lungusa.org/site/pp.asp?c=dvLUK9O0E&b=39853. Downloaded on May 8, 2006.

26. National Center for Biotechnology Information, National Library of Medicine, National Institutes of Health, "Cancers Develop in Slow Stages From Mildly Aberrant Cells." Available online. URL: http://www.ncbi.nlm.nih.gov/entrez/query.fcgi?cmd=Search&db=books&doptcmdl=GenBookHL&term=chemical+carcinogens+cancer+AND+mboc4%5Bbook%5D+AND+374869%5Buid%5D&rid=mboc4.section.4259#4271. Downloaded on May 8, 2006.

27. Henschke, Claudia I., and Peggy McCarty, with Sarah Wernick. *Lung Cancer: Myths, Facts, Choices—and Hope,* New York: W.W. Norton & Company, 2002, pp. 69-71.

28. Ibid., p. 66.

29. Murray, Michael, et al. *How to Prevent and Treat Cancer with Natural Medicine.* New York: Riverhead Books/Penguin, 2002, p. 69.

30. Henschke, Claudia I., and Peggy McCarty, with Sarah Wernick., *Lung Cancer: Myths, Facts, Choices—and Hope,* New York: W.W. Norton & Company, 2002, pp. 68-69.

31. National Center for Biotechnology Information, National Library of Medicine, National Institutes of Health, "The Preventable Causes of Cancer." Available online. URL: http://www.ncbi.nlm.nih.gov/entrez/query.fcgi?cmd=Search&db=books&doptcmdl=GenBookHL&term=preventable+causes+of+cancer+AND+mboc4%5Bbook%5D+AND+374886%5Buid%5D&rid=mboc4.section.4294. Downloaded on May 8, 2006.

32. Wallace, Robert A. *Biology: The World of Life.* New York: HarperCollins Publishers, 1992, p. 23.

33. Henschke, Claudia I., and Peggy McCarty, with Sarah Wernick. *Lung Cancer: Myths, Facts, Choices—and Hope* New York: W.W. Norton & Company, 2002, pp. 62, 82.

34. Wallace, Robert A. *Biology: The World of Life.* New York: HarperCollins Publishers, 1992, p. 623.

35. Ibid., p. 623.

36. Henschke, Claudia I., and Peggy McCarty, with Sarah Wernick. *Lung Cancer: Myths, Facts, Choices—and Hope.* New York: W.W. Norton & Company, 2002, p. 64.

37. Wallace, Robert A. *Biology: The World of Life.* New York: HarperCollins Publishers, 1992, p. 624.

38. Dooley, Joseph F., and Marian Betancourt. *The Coming Cancer Breakthroughs: What You Need to Know About the Latest Cancer Treatment Options.* New York: Kensington Books, 2002, p. 122.

39. Wolfe, Stephen L. *Introduction to Cell and Molecular Biology.* Belmont, Calif.: BrooksCole/Thomson, 1995, p. 655.

40. American Cancer Society. "Tobacco-Related Cancers Fact Sheet." Available online. URL: http://www.cancer.org/docroot/PED/content/PED_10_2x_Tobacco-Related_Cancers_Fact_Sheet.asp?sitearea=PED. Downloaded on May 8, 2006.

Notes

41. American Lung Association. "Lung Cancer Fact Sheet." Available online. URL: http://www.lungusa.org/site/ pp.asp?c=dvLUK9O0E&b=669263. Downloaded on May 8, 2006.

42. Dollinger, Malin, et al. *Everyone's Guide to Cancer Therapy: How Cancer is Diagnosed, Treated, and Managed Day to Day,* 4th ed. Kansas City: Andrews McMeel Publishing, 2002, p. 609.

43. U.S Department of Health and Human Services. *Health Consequences of Smoking: A Report of the Surgeon General,* 2004. Available online. URL: http://www.surgeongeneral.gov/library /smokingconsequences. Downloaded on May 8, 2006.

44. American Lung Association. "Trends in Lung Cancer Morbidity and Mortality." URL: http://www.lungusa.org/ atf/cf/{7A8D42C2-FCCA-4604- 8ADE-7F5D5E762256}/lc1.pdf. Downloaded on May 8, 2006.

45. Henschke, Claudia I., and Peggy McCarty, with Sarah Wernick. *Lung Cancer: Myths, Facts, Choices—and Hope.* New York: W.W. Norton & Company, 2002, p. 64.

46. Pietrusza, David. *Smoking.* Lucent Overview Series. San Diego, Calif.: Lucent Books, 1997, p. 12.

47. Weinberg, Robert A. *Racing to the Beginning of the Road: The Search for the Origin of Cancer.* New York: W.H. Freeman and Company, 1996, p. 23.

48 Pietrusza, David. *Smoking.* Lucent Overview Series. San Diego, Calif.: Lucent Books, 1997, p. 28.

49. Ibid., p. 29.

50. Ibid., p. 31.

51. Douglas, Clifford E. "Nicotine Is Addictive" in *Tobacco and Smoking,* Opposing Viewpoints Series. Williams, Mary E., Tamara L. Roleff, and Charles P. Cozic, eds. San Diego, Calif.: Greenhaven Press 1998, p. 33.

52. Pietrusza, David. *Smoking.* Lucent Overview Series. San Diego, Calif.: Lucent Books, 1997, p. 39.

53. Douglas, Clifford E. "Nicotine Is Addictive" in *Tobacco and Smoking.* Opposing Viewpoints Series. Williams, Mary E., Tamara L. Roleff, and Charles P. Cozic, eds. San Diego, Calif.: Greenhaven Press, 1998, p. 35.

54. Douglas, Clifford E. "Nicotine Is Addictive" in *Tobacco and Smoking,* Opposing Viewpoints Series. Williams, Mary E., Tamara L. Roleff, and Charles P. Cozic, eds. San Diego, Calif.: Greenhaven Press, 1998, p. 36.

55. DeGrandpre, Richard J. "Nicotine Is Not Necessarily Addictive" in *Tobacco and Smoking,* Opposing Viewpoints Series. Williams, Mary E., Tamara L. Roleff, and Charles P. Cozic, eds. San Diego, Calif.: Greenhaven Press, 1998, pp. 37–42.

56. American Lung Association. "Tobacco Product and Advertising Fact Sheet," Available online. URL: http://www. lungusa.org/site/apps/s/link.asp?c=dvL UK9O0E&b=473643. Accessed May 18, 2006.

57. National Cancer Policy Board, Institute of Medicine, and National Research Council. "State Antismoking Programs Work" in *Teen Smoking,* Opposing Viewpoints Series, Haugen, Hayley Mitchell, ed. San Diego, Calif.: Greenhaven Press, p. 45.

58. Epstein, Bruce. "Teen Smoking Is a Serious Problem" in *Teen Smoking,* Opposing Viewpoints Series, Haugen, Hayley Mitchell, ed. San Diego, Calif.: Greenhaven Press, 2004, p. 19.

59. Males, Mike A. "Antismoking Efforts Should Target Both Adults and Teens" in *Teen Smoking.* Opposing Viewpoints Series. Haugen, Hayley Mitchell, ed. San Diego, Calif.: Greenhaven Press, 2004, p. 19.

60. Ibid., p. 7.

61. Farrelly, Matthew C., et al. "Countermarketing Campaigns Can Reduce Teen Smoking" in *Teen Smoking.* Opposing Viewpoints Series. Haugen, Hayley Mitchell, ed. San Diego, Calif.: Greenhaven Press, 2004, p. 42.

62. Ibid., p. 42.
63. Mike A. Males. "Antismoking Efforts Should Target Both Adults and Teens" in *Teen Smoking*. San Diego: Greenhaven Press, 2004, p. 21.
64. Ibid., p. 21.
65. Ibid., p. 35.
66. Henschke, Claudia, I., and Peggy McCarty, with Sarah Wernick. *Lung Cancer: Myths, Facts, Choices—and Hope*. New York: W.W. Norton & Company, 2002, pp. 43–44.
67. Henschke, Claudia, I., et al. "Early Lung Cancer Action Project: Overall Design and Findings from Baseline." *Lancet* 354 (1999): 99–105.
68. Dollinger, Malin, et al. *Everyone's Guide to Cancer Therapy: How Cancer Is Diagnosed, Treated, and Managed Day to Day,* 4th ed. Kansas City: Andrews McMeel Publishing, 2002, p. 619.
69. Scott, Walter, M.D. *Lung Cancer: A Guide to Diagnosis and Treatment*. Omaha, Nebr.: Addicus Books, Inc., 2000, p. 11.
70. Ibid.
71. Ignoffo, Robert, et al. *What Happens in Chemotherapy. Everyone's Guide to Cancer Therapy: How Cancer Is Diagnosed, Treated, and Managed Day to Day.* 4th ed. Kansas City: Andrews McMeel Publishing, p. 71.
72. Ibid., p. 73.
73. Scott, Walter, M.D. *Lung Cancer: A Guide to Diagnosis and Treatment*. Omaha, Nebr.: Addicus Books, Inc., 2000, p. 40.
74. Dooley, Joseph F., and Marian Betancourt. *The Coming Cancer Breakthroughs: What You Need to Know about the Latest Cancer Treatment Options*. New York: Kensington Books, 2002, p. 41.
75. Ibid., p. 25.
76. Ibid., p. 31.
77. Ibid., p. 12.
78. Henschke, Claudia, I., and Peggy McCarty, with Sarah Wernick. *Lung Cancer: Myths, Facts, Choices—and Hope*. New York: W.W. Norton & Company, 2002, p. 248.
79. Murray, Michael, et al. *How to Prevent and Treat Cancer with Natural Medicine*. New York: Riverhead Books/Penguin, 2002, p. 201.

Glossary

adjuvant therapy—Any cancer treatment used after or in addition to the primary treatment

alternative therapy—A healing approach that is not part of the mainstream medical treatment and that is used instead of conventional treatments

alveoli—Groups of microscopic sacs inside the lungs, where the transfer of oxygen and carbon dioxide to and from the bloodstream takes place

amino acids—The basic building blocks of proteins

angiogenesis—The development of blood vessels, necessary for the continuous growth of a cancerous tumor

anti-angiogenesis therapy—A therapeutic approach to starve the cancer cells by cutting off their blood supply

antibodies—Complex proteins manufactured by the white blood cells to fight infection

antigen—A substance, or part of it, that is foreign to the body and stimulates the production of an antibody

antisense RNA therapy—A therapy that introduces RNA into the cell in order to prevent the production of a specific protein known as messenger RNA (mRNA)

apoptosis or programmed cell death—The self-destruction of a cell when it becomes infected or is no longer needed

bases—The four nitrogenous components of DNA: adenine (A), thymine (T), cytosine (C), and guanine (G)

B-cell lymphocytes—Bind to invaders such as cancer cells, bacteria, and viruses, and attack them with the help of T-cells

benign—Not cancerous

biopsy—Extraction of a small sample or tissue from the tumor that will be examined under a microscope to check whether the cells in the tumor are cancerous

blood-brain barrier—Special system of blood vessels that prevents most chemicals from entering the brain

bone marrow—The soft tissue found inside the bones where the blood cells originate

bronchus (pl. *bronchi*)—The large airway that conducts air in and out of the lungs

complementary and alternative medicine (CAM)—See **complementary therapy; alternative therapy**

cancer—Abnormal cells that grow uncontrollably in one site and may invade adjacent tissues and spread to other parts of the body

capillaries—Small, thin blood vessels

carcinogen—Chemical that causes cancer

carcinogenesis—Process of cancer development

cell—Building block of the body

chemotherapy—The treatment of cancer with drugs that kill cells

chromosome—Microscopic structure within cells that carry DNA (the molecule deoxyribonucleic acid). There are 23 pairs of chromosomes in a human cell

chronic obstructive pulmonary disease (COPD)—A combination of the lung diseases chronic bronchitis and emphysema that occurs in smokers

clinical trials—Studies designed to determine if a new treatment is both effective and reasonably safe for humans

complementary therapy—A healing approach that is not part of the mainstream medical treatment and that is used in addition to conventional treatments

CT (computerized tomography) scan or **CAT (computerized axial tomography) scan**—A diagnostic test that uses a computer linked to an x-ray machine to create a series of detailed pictures of areas inside the body taken from different angles

cytokines—Proteins secreted by immune system cells to send messages to other immune cells

cytoplasm—Inside a cell, the fluid outside the cell's nucleus where most chemical reactions take place

de-differentiation—See **differentiation; dysplasia**

diagnosis—The process of identifying a disease by its signs and symptoms

differentiation—The process by which new cells acquire specialized capabilities and characteristic appearances

DNA (deoxyribonucleic acid)—The hereditary material that directs the development and characteristics of all organisms

Glossary

dominant trait—A trait in a pair of chromosomes that is expressed even when only one of the pair carries the gene

doubling time—The time it takes for a group of cells in a tumor to double its number

dysplasia—The process by which cells lose their specialized capabilities and characteristic appearances, and lose differentiation (also known as **de-differentiation**)

epithelial cells—The components of tissue that line hollow organs, all passages of the respiratory, digestive, gastrointestinal, and genitourinary systems, and form the epidermis (skin)

gene—Basic unit of heredity; each gene is a code that is translated and produced into a protein

gene expression—The process by which a **gene's DNA sequence** is converted into the structures and functions of a **cell**

genetic code—The "language" used by cells to pass information to the next generation

genetic susceptibility—Hereditary trait

gene therapy—A treatment that alters a gene

genome—All the genes in the cell; the human genome contains approximately 30,000 genes

hormones—Chemical messengers that play an essential role in the development of the human body

hyperplasia—A rapid increase in the number of cells that occurs early in the development of cancer

immune system—The mechanisms that defend the body against infection and disease

immunotherapy—A treatment that stimulates or restores the ability of the immune system to fight cancer, infections, and other diseases

in vitro—In the laboratory (outside the body), as opposed to in vivo (in the body)

leukocyte—White blood cells that attack germs and other threats to the body, including precancerous cells

lymph—A fluid rich in leukocytes that circulates through a network of lymphatic vessels and bathes the tissues of the body, helping fight infection

lymphatic vessels—A network of thin tubes through which the lymph circulates throughout the body

lymph nodes—Many small oval-shaped organs along the lymphatic vessels where the lymph is filtrated to remove bacteria and other material that could damage the body

lymphocyte—A white blood cell, part of the body's immune system

macrophage—Neutrophils that engulf and eliminate foreign matter, bacteria, and debris from cells that have been destroyed by infection

malignancy—A tendency for an abnormal growth of a tumor to progress in virulence

malignant—Refers to an abnormal growth or a tumor that becomes progressively worse and spreads to other parts of the body (metastasizes)

mediastinum—Space between the two lungs

messengerRNA (mRNA)—Messenger ribonucleic acid; see also **RNA**; **tRNA**

metastasis—The process by which cancerous cells break from the original tumor and migrate to other parts of the body via the bloodstream or lymphatic system; once there, they produce secondary tumor(s)

microorganisms—Living things too small to be seen without the aid of a microscope

MRI (magnetic resonance imaging)—A diagnostic test that uses a magnetic field to capture internal pictures of the body

mRNA—See **messengerRNA**; see also **RNA**; **tRNA**

mutagenesis—The capability to cause a change in the chromosomal DNA

mutation—Any change in the DNA of a cell. Mutations may be caused by mistakes during cell division or by exposure to DNA-damaging agents in the environment

neutrophils—Leukocytes, or white blood cells, that play a role in the early stages of the body's defense against microorganisms

nucleotide—A three-part unit that makes up DNA, each with a sugar, a phosphate, and a base

oncogenes—Mutated or defective proto-oncogenes; they promote cell division like proto-oncogenes, but unlike proto-oncogenes they do not respond to the signals that control cell proliferation. Oncogenes are one of the steps in the transformation of a normal cell into a cancerous one

Glossary

oncology—The study and treatment of cancer

organ—A part of the body that performs a specific function, for example, a lung is an organ

PET (positron emission tomography) scan—An imaging test that highlights areas where sugar metabolism is especially active. Because the metabolism of dividing cells is higher than other cells, it is used to locate cancerous tumors

placebo—A drug or treatment that unknown to a patient in a controlled experiment does not contain any active ingredient

point mutation—Change of a single base in the sequence of the DNA molecule

prognosis—The likely outcome of a disease

protein—Macromolecule (the most complex) with specific three-dimensional structures

proto-oncogenes—Genes that promote cellular growth and multiplication

pulmonary—Related to the lungs

radiation therapy or **radiotherapy**—Use of x-rays to damage or kill cancer cells

recessive trait—A trait that will only be expressed when both chromosomes in the pair carry the necessary gene

recurrent cancer—Cancer that has reappeared after it was believed to have been in remission

remission—Evidence that the cancer has disappeared after treatment

resect—Remove surgically

ribosome—A protein "assembly machine" that works with tRNA to translate mRNA into proteins in the cell

RNA (ribonucleic acid)—RNA serves as the template for the translation of genes into proteins, transferring amino acids to the ribosome to form proteins, and also translating the transcript into proteins

screening—Checking for a disease in people before they have symptoms

somatic cells—Any of the cells in the body, except the reproductive cells

stage—The classification of the extent of a cancer in the body

staging—A universal way of classifying cancer: Staging is usually based on the size of the tumor, whether lymph nodes contain cancer, and whether the cancer has spread from the original site, or metastasized, to other parts of the body

T-cells or **ytotoxic T lymphocytes**—A kind of lymphocyte that recognizes specific antigens in infected cells and kills them

telomere—End section of the chromosome, consisting of repetitive sequences of DNA that are gradually lost each time the cell divides; when the telomere is gone, DNA duplication is impaired and the cell dies

tissue—A group of cells that look alike and have the same function

tissue margin—The border of healthy tissue surrounding the location of cancerous tissue that has been surgically removed or treated by radiation therapy, which was performed to decrease the likelihood that cancerous cells remain

transformation—The changes that a normal cell undergoes as it becomes malignant

tRNA—Molecules that carry amino acids to ribosomes according to mRNA nucleotides

tRNA—TransferRNA; another strand of RNA that assembles a protein by carrying different molecules to ribosomes in the the order specified by messengerRNA; see also **messengerRNA; RNA**

tumor—An abnormal mass of cells that can be benign or malignant

tumor-suppressor genes—Genes that halt cell division, and that can cause cancer when they mutate

vaccine—A substance of killed microorganisms, living attenuated organisms, or living fully virulent organisms administered into a patient to induce immunity to the substances

vein—Blood vessel that carries blood to the heart

x-ray—A form of radiation; used in low doses to diagnose cancer and other diseases; in high doses is used to treat cancer

Further Reading

Books and Articles

Alberts, B., A. Johnson, J. Lewis, et al. *Molecular Biology of the Cell,* 4th ed. New York: Garland Science, 2002.

Coleman, Norman C., M.D. *Understanding Cancer: A Patient's Guide to Diagnosis, Prognosis, and Treatment.* Baltimore, Md.: The Johns Hopkins University Press, 1998.

Diamond, J.W., M.D., and L.W. Cowden, M.D., with B. Goldberg. *Burton Goldberg Presents an Alternative Medicine Definitive Guide to Cancer.* Tiburon, Calif.: Future Medicine Publishing, Inc., 1997.

Dollinger, Malin, M.D., E.H. Rosenbaum, M.D., M. Tempero, M.D., et al. *Everyone's Guide to Cancer Therapy: How Cancer Is Diagnosed, Treated, and Managed Day to Day.* 4th ed. Kansas City, Mo.: Andrews McMeel Publishing, 2002.

Dooley, Joseph F., Ph.D., F.A.C.B., and Marian Betancourt. *The Coming Cancer Breakthroughs: What You Need to Know About the Latest Cancer Treatment Options.* New York: Kensington Books, 2002.

Gaines, Ann, and Jim Whining. *Robert A. Weinberg and The Search for the Cause of Cancer.* Hockessin, Del.: Mitchell Lane Publishers, 2002.

Goldberg, Marshall, M.D. *Cell Wars, The Immune System's Newest Weapons Against Cancer.* New York: Farrar, Straus & Giroux, 1998.

Haugen, Hayley Mitchell, ed. *Teen Smoking.* Opposing Viewpoints Series. San Diego, Calif.: Greenhaven Press, 2004.

"The Health Consequences of Smoking: A Report of the Surgeon General." United States Department of Health and Human Services. URL: http://www.surgeongeneral.gov/library/smokingconsequences/. Downloaded on May 27, 2004.

Henschke, Claudia I., and Peggy McCarty, with Sarah Wernick. *Lung Cancer: Myths, Facts, Choices—and Hope.* New York: W.W. Norton & Company, 2002.

Henschke, Claudia I., D.I. McCauley, D.F. Yankelevitz, et al. "Early Lung Cancer Action Project: Overall Design and Findings from Baseline, C.I." *Lancet* 354, no. 9173 (1999): 99–105.

Lane, William I., and Linda Comac. *Sharks Don't Get Cancer: How Shark Cartilage Could Save Your Life.* Garden City Park, N.Y.: Avery Publishing Group Inc., 1992

Murray, Michael, et al. *How to Prevent and Treat Cancer with Natural Medicine.* New York: Riverhead Books, Penguin Putnam, Inc., 2002.

Pietrusza, David. *Smoking.* Lucent Overview Series. San Diego, Calif.: Lucent Books, 1997.

Rosenberg, Steven A., and John M. Barry. *The Transformed Cell: Unlocking the Mysteries of Cancer.* New York: G.P. Putnam's Sons, 1992.

Scott, Walter, M.D. *Lung Cancer: A Guide to Diagnosis and Treatment.* Omaha: Addicus Books, Inc., 2000.

Wallace, Robert A. *Biology: The Science of Life,* 4th ed. New York: HarperCollins Publishers, 2001.

Weinberg, Robert A. *Racing to the Beginning of the Road: The Search for the Origin of Cancer.* New York: W.H. Freeman and Company, 1996.

Williams, Mary E., Tamara L. Roleff, and Charles P. Cozic, eds. *Tobacco and Smoking.* Opposing Viewpoints Series. San Diego, Calif.: Greenhaven Press, 1998.

Wolfe, Stephen L. *Cell and Molecular Biology.* Hampshire, U.K.: Thomson Publishing Company, 1995.

Web sites

Health information on the Internet is not regulated. A good source to use to evaluate the reliability of medical information on the Web, produced by the governmental agency National Institutes of Health, is "10 Things to Know about Evaluating Medical Resources on the Web" [URL: http://nccam. nih.gov/health/webresources/; updated March 24, 2006].

The best advice when researching the Web is to look first at information from government sites, those with Internet addresses ending in the suffix ".gov"; university medical centers and other educational institutions with the suffix ".edu"; and nonprofit organizations with the suffix ".org." Commercial web sites, those with the suffix ".com," can have subjective agendas that often need verification.

American Cancer Society
http:\\www.cancer.org

American Lung Association
http:\\www.lungusa.org

Web sites

Cancer Care, Inc.
http:\\www.cancercare.org

CancerLinks
http:\\www.cancerlinks.org

CancerNet
http:\\www.cancernet.nci.nih.gov

Centers for Disease Control and Prevention
http:\\www.cdc.gov

Division of Cancer Epidemiology and Genetics
http://dceg.cancer.gov/

Mayo Clinic Health Oasis
http:\\www.mayoclinic.org/

Medical Journals on Yahoo
http://dir.yahoo.com/Health/Medicine/Journals/

MEDLINEplus
http:\\www.medlineplus.gov

Memorial Sloan-Kettering Cancer Center
http:\\www.mskcc.org

National Cancer Institute
http:\\www.nci.nih.gov

National Center for Complementary and Alternative Medicine (NCCAM)
http:\\www.nccam.nih.gov

National Heart, Lung and Blood Institute
http:\\www.nhlbi.nih.gov

National Institutes of Health (NIH)
http:\\www.nih.gov

NIH Office of Dietary Supplements
http://ods.od.nih.gov/

University of Pennsylvania Cancer Center
http:\\www.oncolink.upenn.edu/

University of Texas M.D. Anderson Cancer Center
http:\\www.cancerwise.org

U.S. Food and Drug Administration
http:\\www.fda.gov

Index

Index

Index

About the Author

A Spanish native, Carmen Ferreiro earned her doctoral degree in biology from the Universidad Autónoma of Madrid, Spain. She worked as a researcher for more than ten years in Spain and at the University of California at Davis, and has published several papers in the fields of biochemistry and molecular biology. She has also written three books for Chelsea House Publishers: *Heroin, Ritalin,* and *Mad Cow Disease (Bovine Spongiform Encephalopathy).* She lives in Pennsylvania as an independent writer and translator.

About the Editor

The late I. Edward Alcamo was a Distinguished Teaching Professor of Microbiology at the State University of New York at Farmingdale. Alcamo studied biology at Iona College in New York and earned his M.S. and Ph.D. degrees in microbiology at St. John's University, also in New York. He had taught at Farmingdale for more than 30 years. In 2000, Alcamo won the Carski Award for Distinguished Teaching in Microbiology, the highest honor for microbiology teachers in the United States. He was a member of the American Society for Microbiology, the National Association of Biology teachers, and the American Medical Writers Association. Alcamo authored numerous books on the subjects of microbiology, AIDS, and DNA technology as well as the award-winning textbook *Fundamentals of Microbiology,* now in its sixth edition.